How to Rent a Negro

How to Rent a Negro

damali ayo

Lawrence Hill Books

Library of Congress Cataloging-in-Publication Data

Ayo, Damali.
  How to rent a Negro / Damali Ayo.— 1st ed.
    p. cm.
  Includes bibliographical references and index.
  ISBN 1-55652-573-7
  1. African Americans—Social conditions—1975- 2. African Americans—Social
conditions—1975— -Humor. 3. United States—Race relations—Humor. 4. Satire.
5. American wit and humor. I. Title.
  E185.86.A97 2005
  305.896'073'00207—dc22
                  2005000512

Cover and interior design: Joan Sommers Design

Photographs: Basil Childers, http://basilphoto.com

Photo actors: damali ayo, Annin Barrett, Ayanna Berkshire-Cruse, Amanda
Boekelheide, Floyd R. Cruse, Skeeter Greene, shik love, James Moore, Madeleine
Sanford, Steffen Silvis, Julie Starbird, Kenya DuBois Williams, Rhea Wolf

White noise, the collar, and *card carrying/the race card* are visual works as shown in
damali ayo's gallery shows "shift: we are not yet done," 2001, and "playback," 2003.

© 2005 by damali ayo
All rights reserved
First edition
Published by Lawrence Hill Books
An imprint of Chicago Review Press, Incorporated
814 North Franklin Street
Chicago, Illinois 60610
ISBN-13: 978-1-55652-573-5
ISBN-10: 1-55652-573-7
Printed in the United States of America
5 4 3

"I remember years ago . . . when I would go to a party and I'd be the only colored brother there. And then I'd go to another party, and I'd be the only colored brother there. . . . So now I recognized that there was prime need to be filled here. So I started my famous Cambridge Rent-a-Negro Plan."
      —Godfrey Cambridge, 1964

"Soon, I expect to see a Hertz Rent-a-Negro."
      —Dick Gregory, c. 1965

"You can't just be everybody's rent-a-negro."
      —Mom, 2003

CONTENTS

Acknowledgments

Heartfelt thanks to the following people for making this book, my art, and my life possible:

Bill and Barbara Patterson, Anu Gupta, Meta Valentic, Ben Hill, Richard Tarlaian, Charmelle Green, James Moore, Kim Patterson, Dean Francis, Sarah Davison, Elick and Rachel Patterson, Salome Schwarz, Greg Nigh, Grace Carter, Madeleine Sanford, Chris Gavin, Karen Levin, Toni Hicks, Roberta Wong, Annin Barrett, Angela Taylor, Thom Wallace, Linda Hutchins, William Pope.L, Patricia J. Williams, Dwayne McDuffie, Katharine Mieszkowski, Linda Farris, Jamilla White, Ryan Griffis, Davy Rothbart, Dmae Roberts, Peter Clowney, Studio 360, Miriam Feuerle, Caldera Arts, Regional Arts and Culture Council, Oregon Arts Commission, Mark Woolley Gallery, Roulette Fine Art, Carlton-Hart Architecture, Bill Hart, Julie Mancini, Gard & Gerber, Brian Gard. Special thanks to Hostgator.com.

To Basil Childers and all the photo actors, thank you for sharing your energy and talent.

Thanks to Yuval Taylor and Chicago Review Press for your dedication, openness, and belief in this project.

Special thanks to Marc Gerald for seeing the author in this artist.

LLD and JKM.
Always desperate to sing.

A nod of respect and admiration to all those who came before and to all those who will come after.

Is this you?

You have been working hard at your job for ten years and are ready for a promotion. You're just about to start a conversation about your job advancement when your boss begins to talk about diversity. You wonder, "Is he going to hire a black person to replace me?" You can't risk that. There must be a way to keep your job without ignoring your boss's need for multiculturalism. How can you preempt your boss and impress him at the same time? Then it hits you. What if the next time your company has an open house, you bring a black friend? You can show your boss that you know all about diversity. He won't have to hire a black person after all. He's got you, and you've got your promotion!

Or is this your story?

You treasure your multicultural friendships, but can't keep up with the invitations from friends who want to liven up their social events by adding some local color. You answer so many questions about being black that you're considering writing a handout titled "Blackness 101." At work, you feel like you have two full-time jobs. Not only are you the regional sales representative for your company, you're also the regional African American representative. Suddenly you wonder if you could be charging for these critical billable hours. You think of the days and weeks of unpaid work you've been doing. That extra cash would add up. You could finally take that trip you've been dreaming about!

How to Rent a Negro is here to help.

It's time to bring these two groups together in the spirit of harmony and free enterprise.

Launched in 2003, the popular Web site rent-a-negro.com received thousands of completed rental forms, hundreds of franchising and employment inquiries, and thousands of questions about the specifics of renting. This book evolved to empower individuals and pave the way for a new relationship between renter and rental.

Leaving nothing to fiction, what follows are actual stories, techniques, requests, and responses gathered from over thirty years of research and experience. Each technique listed in this book has been tried and tested by renters and rentals nationwide.

As we all know, the purchase of African Americans was outlawed many years ago. Now, black people are once again a valued and popular commodity. These days those who boast of black friends and colleagues are on the cutting edge of social and political trends. The roles of owner and owned have evolved, preserving the spirit and sanctity of the old relationships without the hassles of long-term commitment, high prices, or their unpleasant features. As we move into this modern context, we can openly discuss this tradition under a new name: *renting*. Those who want to utilize the service of an articulate and well-mannered African American are easily classified as *renters*. Those who find themselves serving as certified African Americans for colleagues and friends are conveniently referred to as *rentals*. These titles allow for imprecise transactions to be clearly defined and newly infused with the vibrant spirit of capitalism.

The practice of renting has been a long-standing tradition since the end of the days of purchase. Renting takes place on a daily basis, virtually at any time, in nearly any location. Unfortunately much of this renting has occurred without the consent or compensation of those being rented. Strained dynamics have plagued race relations for centuries. What better way to alleviate this tension and move into the future than with the honest negotiation of fees for services rendered? Let's talk business. It's the American way.

This guidebook is divided into four easy-to-follow parts. Parts 1 and 3 guide renters and rentals through their respective roles and transactions. Renters learn how to strategically insert black people into social settings, family gatherings, and business affairs to add clout, entertainment, or even controversy. Rentals learn how to craft a profitable career as a rent-a-negro, recouping a lifetime of fees owed. Parts 2 and 4 contain materials such as sample rental applications and real rental experiences that will be of vital interest to members of both groups. This book will serve as a daily resource to both renters and rentals as they study the sections for information about their counterparts. The more you know, the more savvy you'll bring to your side of the transaction.

Ready to start? Read on and you will discover a world of rental techniques, tips, and traditions. In just minutes you'll be on your way to a lifetime of rewarding rental activity!

Baby, I Was Born to Rent

1

Getting Over That Helpless Feeling

It finally happens. There you are, just like every other Tuesday, having lunch with the usual group—friends, colleagues, and local gossips. You share opinions on politics and people. You exchange the standard complaints about the weather and the boredom of work. You admire your ability to withstand it all with a winning smile and a stylish suit. Everything seems perfectly normal, a relaxed routine. Then, as you put down your sparkling water and pick up your cappuccino, you look around and realize that something about this gathering seems particularly pale.

What could it be? Just then the white waiter in his white uniform brings your white pasta, covered by a white sauce that you quickly spill on your white napkin. You look up from the white-on-white stain and examine the faces of your luncheon companions: white, white, white, and . . . white. You are momentarily stunned. You interrogate yourself. "Is everyone I know white?" You stop, this time fully frozen at the thought. "This can't be true. Not *everyone* I know is white." You pause, thinking of a particularly suntanned friend who might emerge as an exception to the monotone. Then you realize, "Darn, he's white too." You think back to your parents' friends. Surely there was an older black person you knew when you were young. No, all of their friends were white as well. You struggle to find the only exception, thinking, "Can I count the cleaning lady who came to our house once a week?"

You ponder hopefully but admit defeat when you realize, "I don't think I even knew the cleaning lady's last name." You take a deep breath. "How did this happen?" you ask yourself. "Has it always been this way and I'm only now becoming aware? How could I be so out of touch, so behind the times?" You've heard all the talk about diversity and multiculturalism and you pride yourself on being in sync with current trends. How did this one pass you by? Your favorite television show used to have all white characters, and now there's a black character on it. You always get the latest fashion ideas from that show, and you don't want to miss out on this new accessory. Maybe you've wondered what it would be like to talk with or be friends with a black person. Your boss keeps saying she wants to increase diversity. Introducing her to a black person might get you that sought-after corner office with the window. Your ex is dating a black person; now you want one of your own. But how do you add this much-needed color to your life? Where do you start?

You are reluctant to bring up your realizations with your white cohorts. You don't know what your friends might think of inserting a black person into their lives. Maybe there's a reason everyone at your lunch table is white. Maybe black people just don't belong in your group. They can be so . . . you know. What if your friends want things to stay the way they are? Will they ostracize you as some kind of renegade, radical, or fetishist? Will they think you've gone too far in your pursuit of the latest fashions? You think back to last month when you showed up at lunch with a new designer briefcase. It was a nontraditional color, and now all your friends have one too. You feel confident that you will be similarly followed in this new trendsetting act. But will they know what to say to a black person? The situation could turn pretty awkward. This idea sounds entertaining. You could have a lot of fun. It could be a great adventure to spice up your social scene with some color, just to show how unpredictable and radical you are.

On the other hand, what if your friends already know black people? Are you the only one with a monochromatic view of the world? You certainly aren't going to point that out. But how do you change the situation with subtlety and style? "How and where can I meet black people?" isn't the kind of casual reference you can ask from a friend, like you might ask for tips on the latest diet, sports bets, or the best cosmetic dentist. You think, "I have to do this on my own."

Know Thyself: Reasons for Renting

Since the purchase of African Americans was outlawed, renting has become a tradition taught and refined through generations. Now that you know that you want a black presence in your life, exactly what kind of presence do you want? Do you want your guests challenged or just entertained? Are you looking to create waves or appear in-the-know? What are your expectations? Renters are as unique as snowflakes. They can be anyone from the wealthiest executive to the most modest worker. Education, economics, geography, age, and gender do not limit anyone from becoming a renter. Use the quotes below to determine what kind of renter you are.

> "He was a pleasant surprise. I expected someone not so calm and endearing."
> —MP, county employee

You might be a renter like MP. When you think of black people, do you think: angry, hostile, too outspoken? Perhaps you need exposure to the kind of black person who can put your mind at ease. You too might be pleasantly surprised at how calm and endearing black people really are.

> "She keeps my life interesting!"
> —MK, auto mechanic

The old adage goes, "Variety is the spice of life." So, many renters find themselves after a rental or two enjoying the excitement that black people add to their lives. Many of these renters turn into life-long customers. Some even begin to develop meaningful relationships with black people. Once you get used to having black people in your life, you'll wonder how you ever lived without them!

"I took him to the country club for lunch . . . all heads turned!"
—TH, executive director

"After seeing me with her, people wanted to know more about ME! I've never gotten so much attention!"
—KL, musician

These two classic renters were enamored of the extra attention they got from having a black person at their side in a public venue. You might be a leader in your profession who wants your peers to see that you can relate to everyone regardless of race. These kinds of public rentals can advance your public image and reputation. You'll be surprised how much more interesting you seem to your friends and colleagues when they find out you know a black person. They will envy your spirit of adventure. Soon they'll be asking you if you rock climb or skydive. Your social calendar will become filled with activities you never dreamed possible. You may even find yourself becoming nominated for public office as "the candidate of the people."

"My only black friend just got the flu and my big party is tomorrow!"
—BK, food server

In a pinch? Running out of black people? Renting can bail you out. You'd hate people to think you don't know any black people just because the ones you know are unavailable.

"We try to diversify while we work on social issues, but we can't do it all!"
—JO, nonprofit board member

Nonprofit businesses are perfect candidates to become rental clients. How can you fight child abuse, terrorism, and environmental decay *and* hire black people? Sometimes even the helpers need a little help.

"I used to worry that I was a racist. Now I know I'm not."
—PS, artist

Sometimes it helps to say you know a black person to show others in your community that you aren't racist. One racist in the neighborhood can make everyone look bad. Don't be that guy.

"Now I understand black people so much better, I want to share the experience with all my friends."
—JJ, convenience store manager

You might be the kind of renter who has a healthy curiosity about all kinds of things, and direct experience is the best way to learn. Do you often find yourself saying, "If I just had a black person to talk to, I could ask them all my questions." Renting has been the answer for many people. This can help end the frustrations you have when interacting with black people in general. Do you always seem to be saying the wrong things? Renting is a great way to practice saying the right things. The next time you talk to a black person, you'll be prepared.

"My generation was different: I didn't know any black people. But my son has a few black friends. Sometimes he seems embarrassed by me because all my friends are white. I can't have my son thinking bad of me. Thank goodness for rent-a-negro!"
—FR, small business owner

All parents want to be up to date and in touch with their kids. One way to do this is by sharing your children's interests. After a few rentals, FR's son is proud to invite his dad and his dad's black buddy to school functions. He is proud to have his friends over to his house for social events. He can know his own black friends will be more comfortable when they see that FR is "down."

"My friends still ask, 'How is that black friend of yours?'"
— TY, physician

TY has taken a popular approach to renting. He meets with a black person for one-on-one informational sessions but attends social events by himself. This way, he doesn't sacrifice any of his well-earned attention. His peers ask about his black friend, but all the focus stays on TY. When black issues come up, TY is quick to share his insight. He proudly interjects, "My black friend says . . . " and all eyes turn to him.

"I'm delighted to show her off. She is a real professional!"
— GB, university president

Having a charity event? White guilt can put your guests in an ungiving mood. Bring a rental who is content, comforting, and easy to talk to. This will reduce symptoms of white guilt and allow people to kick back and enjoy themselves.

"I bring her to my political group meetings. Now we don't have to discuss how to reach out to minority communities anymore. We can talk about real issues."
— AG, grassroots organizer

These days all organizations are being challenged about diversity. Political groups, no matter what side of the liberal or conservative fence they sprout on, need to show that they attract black participants. This can be a pesky and hard-to-resolve issue. Renting makes easy work of this common dilemma and allows your group to focus on the issues central to your mission.

> "Ever since I brought him to my cousin's wedding, everyone in my family thinks I'm a rebel!"
> —RT, college student

Once in a while you get the urge to shake things up with your friends or family. Bringing a black person to the next group event is a surefire way to turn heads and start people talking. Why not have a little fun the next time you have to go to a boring high school reunion or another baby shower? Bring a rental and just wait for the reactions!

> "Black people really are as much fun as they seem in the movies!"
> —KP, delivery truck driver

That black comedian you saw on cable TV last week was really funny. That book your book club just read, by a black author, wasn't half bad. Now you have this inexplicable desire to talk to black people. But you're worried you might not like the first, second, or third black person you meet. Renting lets you try out as many different kinds of black people you want until you find one you are comfortable with.

Frequently Asked Questions (FAQ)

How do I rent a negro?

Many people are already active renters and have been for years. In fact, it is quite common practice for renters to use and reuse the services of black people without permission or compensation. This goes to show that it's not as hard as you might think to enlist a black person for your personal gain. If you are a new renter, start by determining the rental approach best suited to your needs. If you are already renting, it may be time to recognize and refine your technique. Ask yourself, "Have I paid for the services I've utilized or have I just been racking up debt?" Becoming familiar with your rental techniques is the first step on the road to living debt free.

Who is a rent-a-negro?

Most black people are qualified to fill your need for an authentic black presence. Many have a lifetime of experience in the field. As children, black people are often required to introduce black perspectives into schools, neighborhoods, or community groups. Young rentals learn to expertly answer persistent questions about black history, hair, food, culture, and politics. This work continues throughout adolescence and adulthood, cultivating an expertise in the field. By the time many black people are adults, their rental skills have become so fine-tuned, they ought to be held in the same regard as the most well-trained doctors and lawyers, many of whom have only a fraction of the training and hands-on experience of a top-notch rental.

Is renting discreet and confidential?

Absolutely! No one will know you are renting except you and your rental. In fact, renting can be so subtle that you've probably rented already without even being aware of it yourself. Rentals are highly skilled and maintain strict professional confidentiality. Your friends and colleagues will only know what you choose to tell them. Don't worry. They'll be so impressed that you know such interesting people, they'll never suspect you of renting.

What can I expect once I rent?

After approving your rental request, your rental will ask you to sign an agreement and may ask for half the rental fees in advance. Then the rent-a-negro will attend your event and interact according to the expectations outlined in the contract. All you have to do is enjoy your event and the enthusiastic, provocative responses of your guests, friends, or colleagues.

What if I am unsatisfied with my rent-a-negro?

They best way to insure customer satisfaction is to be up front about your rental needs before you rent. It is often the spontaneous rental or the unnegotiated rental that can leave both parties frustrated, unsatisfied, and even wary of renting again. Nip this syndrome in the bud. When you make your rental request, list all your needs in detail. Do you want your rental to argue with your racist grandmother? Make this clear beforehand. Would you rather your rental avoid topics such as racism, affirmative action, and reparations? Better let him know. Do you know if your friends will want a spontaneous dance lesson? Plan ahead so that your rental wears comfortable shoes. Talking about these types of needs with your rental can give you a sense of how well you will work together. You might even find that direct and honest communication can be a lot of fun!

How much does it cost?

Rental services are both practical and affordable, priced per hour and type. Chapter 4 contains some suggested rental rates competitive with other specialty services such as auto maintenance, investment brokerage, electrical repair, and tutoring. Like rental services, it's best to hire a professional for these services because you just don't have the skills to do them yourself.

Certain features may come at an extra cost. These are the little things that make each rental special. For example, will you or your guests want to ask a large number of questions? A high-question-volume fee is standard, much like paying for extra wear-and-tear on a rented tuxedo.

If you can't afford to pay your rental, don't assume he or she will do the work for free. Instead, consider saving up for a rental or combining funds with other members of your community. Group rentals are a common way to introduce the value of black people into a community or social group. At a later date you may be able to afford an individual rental. If your circumstances fit charitable criteria, a rental might consider your appeal as a part of their volunteer pursuits. Many rentals contribute to needy communities through pro bono work.

How does billing work?

Your rental will present you with an invoice (see page 142) that details the agreed-upon services and a fee estimate. Some rentals may accept your personal check or credit card as well as cash.

If you impulse rent (see chapter 6) or have rented without payment or paperwork in the past, there is a possibility that you may be presented with a retroactive bill. Remember the friend you asked a black opinion of last week? You owe him $75 for that. Did you ask your only black friend to mentor a child in your volunteer program? That could tally over $200. Whoops, did you forget to pay for the time you touched a black person's hair? That's another $100 on your tab.

Some rentals offer a reduced rate if you tally your own past-due bill. Take advantage of this. Few creditors would be so generous!

How do I start?

You've probably started already. An effective way to find this out is to ask the black people you know if you are behind in your rental payments. They may already have an account set up for you. Repeat renting is the best way to secure the future services of a rent-a-negro. Simply rehire the people who have already worked for you. You know that they are reliable service providers, so why not give them some repeat business?

But I don't know any black people.

That's why you need to rent! Though black people can be found in almost every region in this country, you may be one of the many people who find themselves at a loss for black connections. Maybe you're even a little scared. Don't worry. There are plenty of ways to fill your rental needs that keep you in the driver's seat. Many renters begin with spontaneous renting: just walk right up to any black person and carry out one of the popular approaches or quickie rentals presented in chapters 4 and 6. If you aren't quite so outgoing, simply place an ad in the local newspaper or a community Web site, or hang some posters around town for the services you seek. Just let your needs lead you. It's easy!

4

Bring It On: Popular Approaches

Following are classic techniques that have been used by renters over the years. They are outlined in easy-to-follow steps. If you are already renting you can check your own methods against those described here. Have you been skipping steps with your rentals? You won't have that problem any more. Now you can follow along to make sure you're renting with the latest well-proven methods. When you use these techniques, you'll show the world that you're a professional renter down to the smallest detail.

Like any long-running tradition, renting has developed its own amusing diversions. Some renters look down on these games while others embrace them wholeheartedly. One playful assignment challenges renters to execute the approaches below without entering into a formal rental contract. Researchers speculate that this fun and furtive ritual is not merely an attempt to avoid paying rental fees. Rather, it is a sporting innovation designed to make renting almost as much as an adventure as buying once was. There is a fee listed at the end of each popular approach. The choice is yours to either pay for what you've consumed or to pull the old rent-and-run.

The Hair Grab

A daily treat! This classic rental method is a favorite, providing renters a constant source of amazement and entertainment. This time-honored tradition began in the nineteenth century, when it was considered good luck to touch the hair of a black person. Contemporary renters have updated this custom by adding curiosity and public spectacle, even making it fun for strangers to join in. It simply never gets old!

Step 1: Always be on the lookout for an exotic-looking African American: you know, one with natural or kinky hair. You can spot one anywhere—in the street, on the bus, at the coffee shop, in the public restroom (a popular spot), in line at the grocery store, at the bar, at your children's school, at a PTA meeting . . . you name it!

Step 2: Keep your eyes on that hair. Walk up to the person. When you get within reaching distance, touch, stroke, pull, fondle, and investigate the hair.

Step 3: Ask, "Can I touch your hair?"

Step 4: Express both fascination and flattery. Say things such as "Your hair is so unique, so strange, I can't resist it!" You might add, "Do you sit around touching your hair all day long? If I were you, I could never stop touching it."

Step 5: Smile at the person. You haven't had this much fun since the Halloween haunted house!

TIME-SAVING TIP

It is common practice not to introduce yourself to the black person. Don't let minor details get in your way. When you get the chance to rent, go for it!

This rental can happen anywhere, in the street, on the bus, at the coffee shop, in the public restroom (a popular spot), in line at the grocery store, at the bar, at your children's school, at a PTA meeting . . . you name it!

Step 6: Continue to have fun touching, twisting, and squeezing the hair. Play with it. Pull it. See if you can tie it in a knot.

Step 7: Loudly, so all nearby parties can hear you, begin a thrilling inquisition about hair and hair care. Popular choices include "How do you get your hair like that?" "Why is your hair that way?" "Can you go to normal salons like me?" "Do you have to do it that way every morning?" "How long does it take you?" "How do you wash it?" "Can you wash your hair?"

Step 8: Don't be selfish. Invite friends, children, and other nearby people to join in by saying: "Have you ever seen anything like this?" "It's so different!" "Don't you agree? It's such interesting hair!" "Go ahead, touch it."

Step 9: Compare the black hair to your hair: "My hair is so boring. It would never do anything like that." Again, volume here is key. Speak loudly so everyone nearby can hear you. Continue to say things like "I've never seen anything like it." "You have to admit it's different. It's strange." Try the classic, "I heard that black people put grease in their hair, like the kind you put in a car. Is that true?" Or a favorite among liberal, organic types, "I had dreadlocks once. I just never washed my hair and it turned into dreadlocks. They were twice as long as yours."

Step 10: When the black person extracts the hair from your grasp, grab it again. She should be flattered by your attention and interest. Remind her that she should respond to your polite interest with polite appreciation.

Step 11: Finally let go of the hair. Wipe your hands on your pants or a handkerchief if you have one handy.

Step 12: Walk away. Continue to express your delight with this hair encounter until you are out of earshot of the black person.

FEE: $100 per hair grab

The Executive Lunch

It's lunch hour. What to do? Why not take the only black employee out to lunch? The town will be talking when they see you two together!

Step 1: Hire a black employee.

Step 2: Scope out the scene at the local restaurants. Where have you always wanted to cause a stir? Choose wisely. Do you want to take your rental to a place where people know you and always give you the best table? Do you choose a spot out of the way, where you might turn heads, but where there will be no rumor to contend with later? Sure, this rental is a fun one, but you don't want it to cause unnecessary damage to your career aspirations.

 **TASTY TIP**

Take your rental to a white ethnic or cultural organization. There, you'll be certain to be supplying the only black person in the room. A favorite spot: the local Italian American social club. Calamari with spicy marinara sauce—delicious!

Step 3: Choose a day when the rental is dressed especially well. Ask him if you can take him to lunch. You know a great place. You'll treat.

Note: Picking up the tab might seem a bit costly, but it's important. That way you will always get to pick the restaurant. You don't want to make this a regular thing. Who knows where he might take you? If you split the bill today, you might have to eat soul food next week.

Step 4: Over lunch, stick to small talk. Steer clear of conversations about social issues. Be careful to avoid any conversations that might lead to the words "tokenization" or "exploitation," or the feeling of being "the only one in the room."

Step 5: Make it clear to the rental that you just want to have lunch. He may think that having lunch with the boss means a raise or a promotion. Be vague and noncommittal during any talk about his career at your organization.

Step 6: While you chat, enjoy the attention garnered from the people around you. Smile and wink at the other patrons. Enjoy your meal. Tip the waiter well.

Step 7: Some time later, when you want an added treat, tell your employee that you really liked having lunch with him because you knew that your eating lunch with a black person would turn heads. And it worked! Thank him for being so much fun to have around. (You might want to save this bit of information until after the employee has given his notice.)

FEE: $200 per hour

Ah, an Expert!

This is a much-loved approach for those concerned about social issues, particularly those who pride themselves on being tolerant, progressive, or even enlightened about race. This approach is popular among busy and thrifty renters. Frugal renters have found that they can reference a singular interaction with a black person for almost an entire year.

Step 1: Attend a social or business event. Realize you have a curious craving to "shake up" the evening or give yourself a memorable experience for the night.

Step 2: As you mingle, keep an eye out for the one black person at the party. (They're probably a rental already. See "I'm Having a Party.") Refresh your drink and get ready to strike up a conversation.

Step 3: Walk confidently up to the black person. If he is in the middle of a conversation, wait patiently while listening in or try to insert yourself into the chat.

Step 4:   Get him to notice you by being witty and personable. There is no need to introduce yourself. Your sense of entitlement will help you to make the most out of this interaction.

Step 5:   Compliment the person by saying, "You look like an interesting person to talk to. When I saw you, I came right over." Compliments are a great way to begin a rental. He may not suspect that you mean, "I want to look fashionable by talking to the one black person in the room."

Step 6:   After a few moments, sway the conversation to a discussion about race.

POPULAR CONVERSATION SWAYERS

"I bet you have an interesting opinion on this, being black and all."

"I was just wondering, is it black, or is it African American? Which do you prefer? I mean, what is the right thing to say these days?"

"I have a situation I bet you could help with . . . there is this woman at my job, and well, she's black. . . ."

"What did you think of [insert recent racially motivated incident of police brutality]? I thought it was just awful."

"What did you think of [insert name of latest black athlete accused of crime]? My friends and I were just talking about it, but I wanted to come over here and find out what you thought."

Step 7: Share all your ideas about race, racism, prejudice, and discrimination. This is your chance to showcase your knowledge and compassion. Solicit the black person's endorsement by repeating, "Don't you agree?"

Step 8: If the black person begins to talk about issues having nothing to do with race, continue to direct the talk back to his black opinions. Be persistent. Press the black person to validate your ideas. Once you feel particularly vindicated, shake his hand and say, "I am so glad I met you."

Step 9: Eventually, the black person may succeed in raising non-race-related topics. Once this happens, finish your drink and walk away.

Bonus Points: You can top off any rental by suggesting that you and the black person get together outside of this social occasion. Hey, you really are progressive! This may be more commitment than you intend but don't worry about your busy schedule getting bogged down. Remember, you haven't even asked his name.

TALKING POINTS

Trying to impress your friends? Renters often choose from these terms to describe their delight with their latest black conversation companion.

Articulate	Well-dressed	Civil
Pleasant	Appropriate	Poised
Well-spoken	Easy to talk to	Polite
Educated	Agreeable	Well-mannered
Calm	Friendly	Well-bred
Composed	Refined	

To really engage your friends, insert the word "surprisingly" before any of these adjectives.

Step 10: For weeks to come, impress your friends and colleagues by telling them how you had a great dialogue with a pleasant and articulate black person. Describe how the two of you talked extensively about race and how you and black people see eye-to-eye on the issue. Use this experience any time race comes up in conversation.

FEES: $75 per black opinion
$1,500 per "Tell them I'm not a racist" vouch

Some of My Best Friends . . .

It is important to put black people at ease in your presence. One way to do this is to show them the other black people in your life.

Step 1: Talk to a black person.

Step 2: After only a few moments find a way to work into the conversation that you know *other* black people. You might introduce this idea with "I know what life is like for you, because my [wife/friend/nephew/neighbor/mailman/nanny] is black."

Step 3: Emphasize how you would like her to meet the other black people in your life. Repeat frequently that you are certain they would all get along and really enjoy each other's company.

HANDY TIP

Keep a photo in your wallet of the black people you know. That way you can pull it out when needed. Surely people will believe that you are trustworthy and understanding if you can show them a photo of your black peeps.

Step 4: If possible, arrange a meeting between this black person and your black person. It's best to do this in a public space where other people can see how connected you are. Make sure you talk up the meeting to both black people. "I can't wait for you to meet each other. You're going to just love each other. You are a lot alike. Really, you're practically twins!"

FEE: $200 per hour

Back from the Beach

All people are just different shades of brown, aren't we? At least, that's what renters claim, again and again. This approach has been used by renters of all ages. Though it's popular among children or children-at-heart, this rental technique remains a favorite for some renters, no matter their age, maturity, or increasing risks of skin cancer.

Step 1: Go on vacation to some place sunny.

Step 2: Get a tan.

Step 3: When you return home, seek out a light-skinned black person (unless you spent an excessive amount of time in the sun).

Step 4: When you see the black person, be very excited. Rush right up to him and begin a conversation about your trip to the beach, desert, third-world country, or wherever you got your tan. Tell him it was the most sunny, wonderful place you've ever been. Explain that you spent so much time in the sun and got *so* tan.

Step 5: Exclaim, "I bet I got *darker than you!!!*"

Step 6: Hold out your arm, pull up your sleeve if necessary. Thrust your arm toward the black person. Say eagerly, "Let's com-

"I bet I got darker than you!!!"

pare!" If he doesn't willingly raise his arm to meet yours, grab it. Pull up his sleeve. Place your arms side by side. Stare at him with an eager expression and say, "See, I *am darker than you*, aren't I?" Say this regardless of how tan you actually are. Smile and laugh in triumph.

Step 7: Continue to insist that you are darker than the black person. Talk incessantly. Nod your head, encouraging his agreement. He may become awkwardly silent.

Step 8: If the black person is reluctant to declare you the victor in the darkness comparison, appeal to other people in the room. Ask them to look at your arm against the black person's. Nod at them and say, "Look! I'm as dark as him, maybe even darker!"

Step 9:   Start a discussion about how you now know what it's like
          to be black, how skin color doesn't mean anything because
          now you are the same color as black people, how people
          thought you were black, or how you wish your skin were
          this color all the time.

          Rain Plan: If your tan has faded by the time you interact
          with a black person, never fear. Simply recall the tanning
          experience by exclaiming, "When I came back from the
          beach last summer, I was so tan, I was *black*! Really, *I was
          black!*" Repeat several times until all of the people in the
          room are either staring at you perplexed or laughing along,
          sharing similar stories.

FEES: $125 per personal appearance
      $100 per skin color comparison
      $75 per skin touch

The Blame Game

"It wasn't me, I swear, it was, uh . . . a black guy." Why face the reper-
cussions of your actions when there's always an easy scapegoat?
Blame a black person. This technique has been tested and proven for
centuries. It's been successfully used by renters of all ages, classes, and
genders. It works for a wide range of questionable acts, from sneaking
cookies from the cookie jar to committing triple homicide.

Step 1:   Commit an illegal, unsafe, immoral, or wrong act of
          any nature.

Step 2:   Get discovered by authorities before you are able to flee
          the scene.

Step 3:   Panic. Your parents, community, and country are going to
          be really disappointed if they find out what you did.

Step 4: Ask yourself, how do other people usually deal with this situation? Have an epiphany when you remember that most Americans think that black people are born criminals. You can easily say a black person did it. Everyone will believe you.

Step 5: Breathe a sigh of relief.

Step 6: Cooperate with the authorities. Present yourself as a witness, not the perpetrator of the act. You are a witness, really—after all, you were there when the negative act was committed.

Step 7: Describe your wrong act in detail. Substitute a black person for yourself. Feel free to embellish—you have everyone's attention and trust.

Alternate plan: This method can also be used as a distraction. You don't have to substitute a black person in your tale of personal wrongdoing. Simply tell any story implicating a black person in any wrong act. You'll look like a hero and the authorities will be hot on the track of yet another societal menace.

Step 8: Want some airtime? Take your story to the media. There's always room for the story of one more black criminal on the evening news. You can even become the "star witness"—remember, you saw everything that happened.

Step 9: Kick back and relax. You're off the hook.

FEE: Various rates apply; determined by situation

You Look Just Like . . .

The old adage goes, "black people all look the same." Renters have proven their faith in this sentiment time and time again.

Step 1: Always be ready. This is another approach that can happen anywhere you spot a black person. Keep your eyes open at school, church, special events, even on the street. If you should spot a black person in a public place, feel free to yell from across the street or from blocks away. They are going to be thrilled to hear your comments.

Step 2: Walk up to her as if you are going to begin a friendly conversation.

Step 3: Open with "*Do you know*, you look just like . . ." You can also try, "Has anyone told you, you look just like . . ." Remember, don't say hello or introduce yourself. Do not offer to shake hands, but feel free to reach out and touch the black person.

Step 4: Insert the name of a famous black person. If you don't know the name of a black celebrity, say, "That woman from that show/movie/commercial. You know the one. The one who looks just like you!" She will know who you mean.

Note: You might want to tailor your choice of celebrity based on the skin tone and hairstyle of the black person you are talking to. Similar hair and skin color are usually enough for renters to declare that two black people are virtual clones.

Step 5: Wait with a broad smile for the black person to thank you for the compliment.

The old adage goes, "black people all look the same."

Step 6: Involve others. "Doesn't she look just like . . . ?" Make this rental a group event.

Step 7: Stand awkwardly close to the black person. Stare at her and wait for the conversation to continue. Or walk away to strike up a substantive conversation with the white person next to you. Both are commonly used techniques.

FEE: $100 per occurrence

Mentoring Works!

We all know how important it is to connect black children with positive black role models. Many black children don't have anyone stable in their lives. Progressive and dedicated renters make the education of black youth a priority. Through their admirable commitment they selflessly provide much-needed mentorship for neglected black youth.

Step 1: Volunteer for a local group that serves children in need.

Step 2: Feel sympathy and pity for the only black child in the group. As you discover that black children have special needs, decide that she needs someone just like her in her life.

Step 3: Do not find out whether the black child has any specific skills or interests she would like in a mentor such as writing, carpentry, business, classical music, etc.

Step 4: Wrack your brain to think of the one black person you know. This may be your only black friend, or the only black friend of one of your other friends—your black friend once removed. Don't consider this a problem. Say to yourself, "She'll understand. She knows what it's like to be an 'at-risk' child."

Step 5: Call the potential black role model at home in the evening.

Step 6: She may be initially surprised at your call. Use this to your advantage. Start by saying, "I was thinking of you recently," then move right into your plea. Tell her about the special youngster you met in your program. Proclaim that the needy child and the potential mentor have so much in common and would naturally take a liking to each other. When the mentor-to-be feigns polite interest at this remark, swoop in with your proposal that she mentor the child. Remember to mention that this child needs someone black in her life because you simply cannot relate to the child's needs.

Step 7: You start to make some progress. She might consider meeting the child, despite her busy schedule. She says she would like the two of you to get together for a friendly lunch. Don't panic. Steer the conversation back to mentorship and how important it is to provide community for needy black children. Don't get distracted. If you find this child a black mentor, you will gain the respect of everyone in your organization.

Step 8: If the black person still sounds uninterested, up the stakes by describing how hard you've tried to meet the child's needs: "I try to take the group to black movies, but all the other girls are white and I have to take their interests into account. I can't spend all my time focused on one girl's issues." Emphasize again how the child needs someone *like them*. Restate how you just don't have the time, ability, and most importantly, the skin color to be a useful mentor to a black child. You might add, "She's completely disconnected from her heritage and what it means to be black."

Step 9: Should all else fail, feel free to recite some of the black phrases you've heard with regard to community. Perhaps this will induce guilt and a commitment. Some suggestions include "each one, teach one," "give back," "remember your roots," and "it takes a village to raise a child." If all else fails, remind the black person that she could never have accomplished all she has in her life without the help of positive black role models.

Step 10: Return to your volunteer organization and announce with pride that you recruited a black mentor for the child in need. Remember to tell the child that you've found the perfect mentor for her. Tell her how excited she'll be when she sees her new mentor.

FEES: $200 per hour
$1500 per "Tell them I'm not a racist" vouch

"I read this book about black people and I just know you'll love it!"
It's always nice to demonstrate to black people how in touch you are
with black culture. Maybe you're even more in touch than they are.

Step 1: Read a book by a black author.

Note: If you don't have time to do this, just think back to
high school. There's no need to read more black authors
than you have to. Most high school curriculums integrate
a black book or two into the reading list, usually during
February. Remember? Great. Need to jog your memory?
It was the one about poverty, squalor, urban strife, addic-
tion, and crime.

Step 2: Talk to a black person.

Step 3: As you search for things to discuss, bring up the book
you remember. It was written by a black person, or was it
about black people? Anyway, it had something to do with
black people.

Step 4: Insist to the black person that you are certain that she
would enjoy reading this book. You may not know
anything about the black person or her interests. That's
fine, just describe how the book relates to her life and
that you would love to talk with her about it. You know
her opinion about the book would be so interesting.
In fact, you may still have a copy of the book if she wants
to borrow it.

Step 5: Repeat step 4 several times.

Step 6: After you've told her repeatedly that the book is perfect for
her, ask if the person has read the book. If she has read it,
be surprised. You know you *should* think that black people
are intelligent, but it always catches you off guard to meet

one who actually is. If she has not read it, be surprised. After all, the book is about her people. Look at her in disdain as you wonder if she is really as black as you thought.

FEE: $200 per hour

HANDY SHORTCUT

In any situation where you are referencing a black author, actor, sports figure, or politician, use the opportunity to display your comfort with black people in general. An easy way to do this is make sure you refer to the star only by a first name. Never use last names and avoid using titles like Dr., Mr., Ms., or Mrs. Just say Condi, Denzel, Tiger, or Jesse. Talk about this black celebrity as if you know them personally.

Insist to the black person that you are certain that he would enjoy reading this book. Explain how the book relates to his life and that you would love to talk with him about it.

Movin' On Up . . .

Why limit renting to one or two black people? This approach lets you rent an entire black neighborhood! The newest, freshest, hippest, and yes, cheapest neighborhoods to move into these days are those populated by black people. Here's your step-by-step guide to perfecting the modern trend of urban gentrification.

Added bonus: this approach opens new avenues for future renting (see step 10).

Step 1: Get ready to move. Maybe your family is expanding and you can't afford to get a bigger place in your current neighborhood.

Step 2: Investigate moving to the predominantly black neighborhood in your town.

Step 3: Drive through the neighborhood slowly, inspecting all the available homes, even some that aren't yet available.

Step 4: Worry when you wonder if you will be able to relate to your new black neighbors. Smile when you realize this will be a chance to put your progressive community values into action. Breathe a sigh of relief when you hear that other white people are scoping out the neighborhood just like you are.

Step 5: Move in and drive up property taxes.

Step 6: Boast about your funky new digs. Tell all your friends that you live in the "'hood." Invite them to come visit you when they feel like "slummin'."

Step 7: Encourage your friends to join you in your new neighborhood. Maybe they can open a business there. Space is affordable and the neighborhood could use some fixing up. Wouldn't it be great if you could get your morning coffee right around the corner?

Step 8:   When someone challenges you about your choice to dis-
place black families, refute this charge by saying, "Where
else was I supposed to live? It was all I could afford. Do you
think I would *choose* to live there? The people *wanted* to
move out of their place. I didn't force anyone to leave."
Dismiss associations people make between your behavior
and colonialism.

Step 9:   Plot out several routes to work as you try to avoid driving
by the low-income housing that is being built for the
people who used to live in your home.

Step 10: See other rental techniques. Now that your neighborhood
doesn't have any black people, you'll have to import some
for special occasions.

FEE: $12,000 per year

| **Chocolate Is My Favorite Flavor!** |

Brown and creamy, sweet and sinful, chocolate is a delicious treat. But
don't indulge too much or you might get hooked. You know what they
say, "Once you go black, you never go back." Many renters are curious
to find out if this popular adage about black sexuality is true. What
better way to investigate the rumors than having a taste yourself? It's
a bit like bungee jumping. You may only try it once in your lifetime.
After that you can bury the experience in your past or bring it up as
an exotic escapade retold in the occasional game of "I never." But pro-
ceed with caution. A few renters become bona fide chocoholics.

Step 1:   Date a black person.

Step 2:   Go out often. Take your new lover to restaurants, bars, and
open-air concerts. Be conspicuous together in public as
much as you can.

Step 3: When you are in public, kiss frequently, touch, caress, and stay in contact at all times. Maximize your public displays of affection—you want to make it clear to everyone that you two are *intimate* partners.

Step 4: Savor the attention as all eyes in the room turn to see you kiss your black lover. Some curious onlookers may be turned on by the display. Others might be disgusted. Regardless of the nature of the attention, enjoy it. You feel like a celebrity!

PLAYFUL TIP

Give your black lover a skin-colored pet name. Pet names that reference food are quite popular with renters. Brown Sugar, Cocoa, Sexy Spice, and Cinnamon are popular choices. Choose a name that sounds enticing as well as flattering. It might even make you both . . . hungry.

Step 5: When you are with your friends, casually mention that you are dating a black person. Work this tasty bit of information into every conversation in a subtle way, making sure the conversation ultimately turns to you and your new fling.

Step 6: When your friends ask what it's like to date a black person, say, "I don't get hung up on those labels."

Step 7: Make room in your social calendar for double dates. Your friends will want to be seen with you and your new squeeze.

Step 8: Wherever you and your lover go, comment to him or her about how people stare at the two of you. Say how you bet other people would *never* put the two of you together and how strange you must look as a couple. Whenever you make these comments, remember to follow it up with a smile, a kiss, and "I think it's great. You're so beautiful. I bet they all wish they could have you."

Step 9: Relax. Now that you're dating a black person, you're obviously not racist.

Step 10: When your lover and you experience prejudice, dismiss it. For example, when the two of you get seated at the back of a restaurant, when a hotel clerk says there are no rooms available, when your lover is followed by department store security, or when someone at the table next to you makes a joke about colored people. Simply ignore these things. If your lover gets upset about these incidents, say, "You're imagining those things. I'm sure it wasn't because you're black." Comfort your partner's worries by saying you want to have sex.

Step 11: One evening as you sit having dessert by the fire, your black lover may want to talk with you about race issues. When this happens, hold hands, look deep into the big eyes you're always complimenting, and say, "I don't think of you as black."

Step 12: When the relationship ends, don't take any responsibility for the breakup. If anyone asks why you don't have that black lover anymore tell them, "[He/She] was too uptight for me, so focused on our differences. I thought we had so much in common, but [he/she] just can't see people as people."

FEES: $200 per hour
$1500 per "Tell them I'm not a racist" vouch
$500 per racist family member challenged

I'm Having a Party!

And I really want you to come! Parties are a great way to show off your personality. Displaying your connection to black people is part of keeping an impressive social profile. But wait! What if you aren't friends with any black people? What then? Never fear. You're a person of great charm. You may not have black friends, but you like black people. You're confident that with your invitation and a little flattery the black person you met last month would be happy to attend your gathering.

Step 1: Plan a party. It could be for a special occasion, a sporting or political event, or just to show off your new kitchen and your impressive social network.

Step 2: Make your invitation list. Realize there are no black people on it.

Step 3: Panic. Chastise yourself for being a closed-minded, hypo-critical, all-talk-no-action, armchair liberal.

Step 4: After a short self-flogging, take a deep breath. Remind yourself that you are one of the most open-minded people you know. Remember how you volunteered last Thanksgiving at the homeless shelter? Most of those people were black and you fed them just like everyone else. You smiled at them, even chatted. You are not a racist. Never in a million years could anyone accuse you of that. Eschew the thought.

Step 5: Think hard. You must know one black person somewhere. Have a glorious epiphany when you remember how friend-ly you are with that black clerk at the grocery store. You'll invite him! He'd love to come. Will he know what to say to the other guests? He works at the natural food store. He can talk to your guests about organic produce. But what will he wear? You've only seen him in his store uniform. You hope he has decent taste in clothes. He's so beautiful

You must know one
black person . . .
somewhere.

to look at, it might not matter what he wears anyway. Oh, but your spirit of innovation takes over. You'll have a casual gathering. Maybe even a barbeque. Black people love those, and there's no pressure to look nice or talk about anything sophisticated. He'll fit in just fine.

Step 6: Go to the grocery store on short missions. You have to catch the clerk when he's working. Maybe you can ask his advice on some dishes for the party, even find out what he likes to eat. Be sure to find out when he's free and plan your party for a time when he can attend. What is his name? Make a mental note to look at his name tag.

Step 7: Once the party date is set, take an invitation with you to the grocery store so you can give it to him in person. Inquire as to whether he's ever socialized with any of his other customers. You want to be the first. Your friends will be so impressed when they see him there. Imagine, asking the grocery clerk to your home!

Step 8: Plan several more trips to the grocery store between now and the party. Each time, remind the black clerk how much you're looking forward to his attending the party. Tell him that you really want him to be there. Emphasize that he'll have a great time and that he'll enjoy meeting your friends, though he might find them a bit stuffy, since you're sure they won't be anything like his friends or the people he's used to hanging out with. Emphasize that his presence at the party is the one you're looking forward to the most. Say this often.

Step 9: Tell all of your friends to be sure they come to your party. Tell them this is an event they won't want to miss because you've invited some really interesting people. Make certain to invite your friends who you think can chat comfortably with a black person. Call people who have an interest in ethnic food, jazz music, and charity work. Call that friend who went to Africa on vacation last year.

◇ **PRACTICAL TIP**

Renters have found repetition to be a central part of communicating with black people. This way your rental will be sure to understand your words and feel your genuine sincerity. You'll also find this technique commonly used with children and recent immigrants.

For extra fun: Be sure to invite the people who might be uncomfortable around someone black. Later you and your friends can laugh about their awkwardness. Wasn't it funny when those guests left the party early?

Step 10: When the black person arrives, say loudly, "I'm so glad you could make it!" Compliment his clothing. Lead him through your party as you introduce him to every single person there. Show how comfortable you are with black people by calling him by a nickname, touching him a lot, laughing at everything he says, and asking his opinion on every subject that is discussed. Try to keep him by your side as often as you can.

Step 11: During the party spend as much time as you can either talking with the black person or talking about the black person. Don't let him out of your sight.

Step 12: When your friends pull you aside and ask, "Where did you find this interesting man?" tell them that you've known him a long time. You frequent the same food establishment. If you are feeling more honest, go ahead and divulge that he is your grocery clerk but that you have been friendly for quite a while and you see no reason to distinguish between "types" of people in your life. You feel it's important to treat everyone the same.

Step 13: After the party the black person may invite you to lunch or dinner. Feign interest, but decline. You wouldn't want to be seen eating a meal together in public, just the two of you. Who knows what people would say? You know what everyone says about black men. They'd probably think you were having an affair!

FEE: $200 per hour

Note: Other services may be accumulated during the course of the party. Keep a running tab.

I'm Having a Party! (Kids Version)

This popular version of the party technique can involve the whole family. This rental can increase your status in your community without the nasty trouble of having to interact with any adult black people. Children can be a great substitute for adults, and they still count as black. It's a handy approach, especially if you are the type of renter who says, "I think black children are so cute!"

Step 1: Your child (age three to twelve) is having a birthday. Suggest that it would be great to have a party for your child and all of their friends.

Step 2: As you help your child plan the party, decide a theme, and decorate the house, make sure you have a significant say in the invitation list. Who you invite can make a difference in your own social circles, even if the guest list only includes kids.

Step 3: Insist that your child invite a black friend from school, an extracurricular activity, church, or wherever you can find one. Be cautious not to invite too many—you don't want your party to be overrun with black children. Who knows the damage they might do?

Do you know a brother-sister team of black children your child's age? You might want to invite them. This tactic is especially effective for dodging the argument that you are tokenizing black people by only inviting one. You may worry, "What if my child isn't close with any of the black children in the community?" Never fear, invite them anyway. You can convince your child that either (a) they might like the black kids or (b) it's only for this one party.

Step 4: Have your child deliver the invitation to the black child (or siblings) directly. This assures that you avoid all contact

◇ THOUGHTFUL TIP

> Always include an easy-to-follow map with your party invi-
> tation. This will probably be the first time the black parents
> have visited your neighborhood. They will need to know
> how to get to your house. Put brightly colored balloons on
> your door in case they get lost. But what if they use the map
> to drop in for a friendly surprise visit some day when they're
> in the area? Don't worry. Do you drop by their house when
> you're in their neighborhood?

with the black parents, which might result in an awkward
invitation to dinner or cocktails with the adults.

Step 5: At the party, make sure that you give the black child
(and any siblings) lots of attention. It's important for your
social image that the child report to other people that
he or she had fun at your house.

Step 6: Single out the black child for games, activities, and conversation. If you have a sibling pair, mix them in among the
other children. You don't want your party to look segregated.

Step 7: Show extra concern for the black child (or siblings). Ask,
"Can you eat this? Have you ever had birthday cake before?
Do you have games or books at your house?"

Step 8: Show a fun kid's movie, something you loved as a child,
a part of your culture you want to share, perhaps *Willy
Wonka and the Chocolate Factory*, *Grease*, or an animated
Disney classic (you know, the one where the princess is
white as cotton and the evil witch is black as dirt. Or the
one where the main character has to give up her identity

to be accepted by the popular, more powerful group. Or the one where the main character realizes he just isn't like anyone around him, and so is outcast. Just about any Disney movie will do.) Any of these films are sure to make a lasting impression on the black child.

Step 9: If another child at the party says something that might sound racially offensive, reprimand the child in front of the whole group. Make it clear that no one should say those kinds of things in front of the black child or children in the room.

Step 10: When the party is over, tell the black child (and any siblings) that he or she is always welcome in your house. Send the poor thing home with a generous party favor. For extra credit, offer the child one of your own kids' old coats, sweaters, or toys. If your child complains, explain that black children always need a handout, then take your child shopping to buy another.

FEE: $200 per hour

Note: It might be a bit awkward to pay a child for rental services. Instead of finding yourself in this unsightly arrangement, why not establish a trust fund in the child's name? You can make direct deposits with each new rental. This comes in handy for repeat rentals, either by you or other families. Once a child is rented for one birthday party, they are often rented for many birthday parties in the community due to referrals from other satisfied renters.

Common Ground

"I have this great idea for a project but need a black person to do it with. Hey, what about that black woman I met a few times recently?" This approach is usually implemented after you've made the acquaintance of a black person—after you've met them at least twice. Use the one or two things you know about them to make this rental the most effective.

Step 1: Spot the black person in a public setting, like a café or bookstore. This interaction is most effective if the black person is alone and you can capture her entire attention. If she is at a café, feel free to sit down at her table and stay as long as you want.

Step 2: Greet the person. "Hi, how are you doing? Do you remember me?" Sit down with her. "Can I sit down? I was hoping I would run into you. I have so much I want to talk to you about." Order a drink as the waiter passes by. "In fact, there is this idea I have for a project that I think you will be really interested in."

Note: In this approach you might need to remind the black person of your name, but do not make the mistake of sincerely asking her permission to chat or join her. Give her no opportunity to maintain her personal space.

Step 3: When you are comfortably settled at the table with the black person, begin to describe your idea. It might sound something like this: "I was thinking because I am a [fill in your profession] and you have such a different perspective on things, that we should do a project together. I know it would be great, really fascinating because I'm white and you are black, so there would be two really different perspectives. I know everyone would want to see how differently we see things. I think everyone would be interested in this project. We could take it to the newspaper and see if they would do an article on it."

Step 4: When the black person responds that she is already working on several projects, reiterate that your project would be unique and socially important because you are white and she is black. Clearly she has never thought of pursuing such collaboration before.

Step 5: Don't take no for an answer. Continue to press, pursue, and persuade the black person to agree to work with you on your vision of intercultural collaboration.

Step 6: You convince her to consider your idea. She may simply be offering you polite interest in the hopes of getting back to drinking coffee and reading the newspaper. Don't worry; you just need her to say she will consider it.

Step 7: Thank the black person and continue about your day. There's no need to follow up on the collaboration. Instead, use the black person's name frequently in conversations with your friends and colleagues. You might say, "She and I had a meeting. We're going to work together." Your friends will be both impressed and envious.

Note: It's common to discover that your friends, out of envy for your cross-race project, have rented their own collaborator and are poised to pursue a similar project. In this case you may need to follow up with your rental. This is unlikely, though, since your friends are probably following this same rental technique.

FEE: $200 per hour, including any hours actually devoted to the project

The *N* . . . *N* . . . *N*-Word

Black people can be so sensitive about language. It can feel difficult to know what to say or not say in front of them. For example, have you always been afraid to say the *n*-word in front of a black person? You're not the only one. Thankfully, there is an easy solution to this recurring dilemma. Many renters have found clever ways to work the *n*-word into conversations. This tried-and-true approach lets you say "nigger" all you want without being persecuted for being racist.

Step 1: Read an article or book or listen to a news story or song in which someone uses or discusses the word "nigger." Some suggestions include news broadcasts about hate crimes, a range of recordings from musicians and comedians, and many of the books praised as classic works of American literature.

Step 2: Find a black person to talk to.

Step 3: Strike up a conversation about the article, event, song, or book you've just digested. When you get to the part where the *n*-word comes in, use it freely and frequently. It's all in context.

Example 1:
"In the book *To Kill a Mockingbird* they call that lawyer, Atticus Finch, a 'nigger lover' just because he was trying to help a black person. I thought that was awful. To call him a 'nigger lover.' I mean it took a lot of courage for him to stand up for a black person like that. 'Nigger lover!' How horrible. But that's how things were back then, people said things like 'nigger lover.' And this novel is very realistic. It shows how things were in those days, when people would do that, call someone a 'nigger lover.' I mean back then, they just didn't care. Now we can't go around calling people 'nigger lovers.' We'd get arrested."

Example 2:
"I saw this black comedian on a cable special and he used the word 'nigger' over and over again. He was calling himself a nigger, calling other black people niggers. I was shocked. To hear him say 'nigger' over and over like that, 'nigger, nigger, nigger.' I'd never heard anything like that before. But I guess you all can say that to each other. 'Nigger,' I mean. If I said 'nigger' to a black person, I'd get in so much trouble."

Example 3:
(This technique can also be used with "colored" or "negro.") "Have you seen that book, *How to Rent a Negro?* The book is all about how people can rent a negro for their personal use. There are all these negro rentals, negro tips, negro business cards, negro forms, negro letters, and a negro quiz. It is so funny. It says stuff like if you were the only black person in a room you'd be a rent-a-negro. Like right now. You're kind of a rent-a-negro right now. What does that feel like? Anyway, you have to read this book to believe it. People actually rent negroes! Wow. I would never do anything like that, ever."

FEE: $200–350 per hour; dependent upon setting

5

Tools of the Trade: Renter Resources

Some may say that renting is an art form or a finely honed craft. The language, methods, and mental discipline that go into successful rental techniques have certainly been cultivated over the years. If you aren't quite the Rembrandt of renting, these basic tools can help. If you want to be a first-rate renter, don't leave home without them.

You're So Articulate! Handy Terms

Tongue-tied? Tripping over your words? Never fear. These terms will come in handy for every new or seasoned renter.

acquaintance: *n.* A person whom you know on a peripheral basis. Not an intimate connection. You may only have met this person once or twice, often in a group setting. You only know a few personal details about his or her life. It is common to only know a first name. Rental-renter relationships commonly begin between people who are acquaintances. This initial interaction offers the renter a chance to observe and evaluate the rental in a range of social settings before making a formal proposal to rent.

African American: *n., adj.* A term used to denote Americans of African heritage. Controversial because people can find the term cumbersome. Many complain that "It just takes too long to say." Others maintain that the term is an ethnic identification that excludes other black groups (e.g., Antiguan American, Afro-German, or Jamaican English), many of whom share similar racial experiences.

authentic: *adj.* A term meaning unquestionably real. Did you rent a real black person or some kind of imposter? This can be a pesky question. You can ask your rental to show you their credentials if their word and skin color is not proof enough. Black people are identified as such when they enter this country though immigration or birth. There are many easily accessible documents that can prove a person's blackness. (See "certified at birth.")

black: *adj.* A term used to denote people of African descent around the world. The term relates to both skin color and heritage. It can be confusing to renters because people ranging from the very dark to the very light are included in the category. Also confusing due to the word's association with all things negative. Common dictionary definitions include: "evil," "dismal," "gloomy," "wicked," "extremely dishonorable," and "causing misfortune." This can cause a person to hesitate when using the term to describe a human being; as a result, the term is frequently whispered.

certified at birth: *adj.* Documented to satisfy qualifications or standards. In the United States and many other countries, race is listed on one's birth certificate. Race is also listed on immigration records and many job, school, and service applications. Should you have any doubt about the authenticity of a black person, you can refer to these documents for proof of his or her racial identity.

friend: *n.* A person in your life with whom you share history, feelings, trust, concern, and life's intimate details. Friendships take time to develop and are mutually fulfilling on an emotional level. Many say a good friend is a treasure and should be treated as precious. Though renters often refer to current and past rentals as "my friend," this is simply a term of convenience designed to preserve the natural appearance and confidentiality of a rental agreement. Renter-rental relationships should not be confused with friendships.

invoice: *n.* Also referred to as a bill. A document detailing services and payment. Often given as part of a business transaction, like a rental. Usually kept on file with both payer and payee. Copies of invoices can serve as proofs of purchase and proofs of delivery.

Popular in small-claims court cases. (A sample invoice for rent-a-negro services can be found on page 142.)

negro: *n.* A term used for many years to denote a person of the black race. Modern usage is generally derogatory. Historically, black comedians have used the term in a satirical manner that acknowledges its derogatory impact. Though this can provoke laughter among groups of all kinds, when used by nonblacks (or those with unrefined comedic skills) the result can be awkward or offensive.

race: *n.* A distinct group of the world's population differentiated by inherited physical attributes, genealogy, and sometimes shared history. General standards as well as official practices commonly assign at least one race to a person. However, more than one racial category can sometimes be assigned to an individual. Though scientific and social definitions of race remain under constant debate, society continues to lean heavily on accepted racial categories. Countries, families, and social and political groups frequently describe, count, and divide their members according to race. This fixation is evident in the common practice of ascribing characteristics belonging only to a few individuals to an entire race. Thus, the phrases "I don't see race" and "I don't really have a race" may be more accurately translated as "I need glasses" and "I don't like to admit that I'm white."

racism: *n.* The mistreatment of a group of people by members of the power-holding group of a society. Perhaps the most controversial of all terms in the modern vernacular; sometimes referred to as the *r-word*. It remains one of the most heinous of invectives in any political arsenal. As such, it is frequently used for extreme cases of media slander and political sabotage. Though people's ability to perpetrate racism is directly linked to their historical and social power, this term has been subject to various and sundry creative recharacterizations. These include the fictive "reverse racism," the perplexing "positive racism," and the mythical "black-on-black racism." Many governments worldwide continue to debate whether the perpetration of racism should be treated as a crime or merely bad manners.

racist: *n.* A person engaging in racism. Frequently used in a negative manner. Often heard in the phrase "I'm not racist." This comment commonly follows a race-based action or comment. This phrase is also common when the person speaking is concerned that his or her action may have a negative impact. It is frequently used as a preface before telling a story or joke involving an unpleasant depiction of a racial group.

rent: 1 *v.t.* To utilize services, equipment, or space on a temporary basis without purchasing, owning, or making a long-term commitment.

2 *n.* The amount of money given in exchange for the temporary use of a service or commodity.

rental: *n.* An item or person utilized in a situational and temporary fashion. Also, an event or occasion during which a service or item is rented.

renter: *n.* A person who temporarily utilizes an item or person.

token: *n.* A colloquialism used to denote a singular black person purposely inserted into a situation for the purpose of adding variety, diversity, or racial novelty. Though a rental is usually a token during a rental event, most black people do not like to be referred to by this term. However, the term is sometimes used among black people in private when recapping their day's activities. Also used as a verb to describe the singling out of one black person as the race's representative in a group or organization: to *tokenize.*

retroactive billing: *n.* This can occur when rental services have been rendered and fees accrued but the services have not been paid for. A retroactive bill (invoice) can be issued at any time. If you receive a retroactive bill, pay it at once. Debt is one of the main problems plaguing the global economy.

white: *adj.* Descendents of European and some Semitic peoples. Confusing due to the word's association with all things good. Common dictionary definitions include, "the color of pure snow," "angelic," "clean," and "without malice." Despite these positive associations, when applied to a person, the term often raises discomfort among people belonging to this racial category. Many prefer to reject this label in favor of a less controversial ethnic identity. The kind of response often heard from a person identified as white is, "I'm not white, I'm Irish."

white escort: *n.* A white person accompanying a rental. In some settings, a rental may find the presence of an escort helpful. It is the job of a white escort to intervene should the situation threaten the safety of the rental. Conveniently, a white escort can blend into the setting without drawing attention away from any rental action.

Check You Out: A Checklist for the Prospective Renter

Still unsure if you are the renting type? This checklist of tools is handy if you are wondering, "Am I really a renter?" Ask yourself, "Am I using the tool?" If you answer, "yes," then you are probably already participating in the trade.

☐ **Good Intentions**

> "I'm not a mean person. I am kind. I respect people. I like everyone. Everyone tells me I'm one of the nicest people they know. No one would ever accuse me of trying to use another person. I would never try to hurt anyone. I'm not insensitive. In fact, compared to most people, I'm harmless."

This mantra's frequent prayerlike repetition has made it one of the most popular and essential renter's tools: the renter's "Hail Mary." It is also common for this tool to be utilized postrental, often when the renter is faced with a bill for services rendered. Unfortunately, few professionals accept good intentions as a substitute for payment. So be careful, you don't know where your good intentions might lead you. Remember, your mother always said, "The road to hell is paved with good intentions."

☐ An Unflappable Faith in Your Respect for Black People

"I'm not a racist! I like black people. I find them so interesting. I have black friends. Well, I had a black friend once. I mean, I knew a black person. When I was a kid there was one in my school. Anyway, I know *you* and you're black. Just because there aren't any black people in my environment, doesn't mean I don't want to know any. It's hard for me. It takes so much effort to get to know black people. But that doesn't change how much I love and respect black people. They are all so interesting, unique, so . . . different. Black babies are so cute! I love things that are different. I always try different kinds of food when I go to a restaurant. I'm not afraid of things like that."

Of course you like black people. Everyone knows that. Really, would you rent a car that you didn't like? Of course not. In fact, you purposely rent the car that you really do like but can't afford to buy. Owning is a big commitment, requiring payments and maintenance. Maybe it's not a practical, everyday kind of car. Your lifestyle just can't accommodate something that racy. What would the neighbors think?

☐ A Sense of Entitlement

"What did I do that was so wrong? What is the big deal? I treat people nicely, that should be enough. I have a right to be who I am just like you want to be who you are. Why should I change just to accommodate someone else? You want me to understand, right? So, when I ask you a question, you should want to answer me. We've done so much to help black people already."

Entitlement is a precious legacy passed down through generations—beginning with the founders of this country. Today a national sense of entitlement allows our country to be the leader of the free world. You'll find your natural sense of entitlement will come in handy in all rental situations. Nurture your entitlement—after all, you were born with it.

☐ A Well-Rooted Double Standard

"Curiosity is healthy. I wouldn't mind if someone showed an interest in my culture. But black people look at me like I'm from the KKK. I mean, in other places in this country there is *real* racism. Here, it's easy. People are at least interested in each other. It could be much worse. Black people are so sensitive. They get defensive and shut the whole conversation down. How will we ever learn to appreciate each other if black people keep getting offended? That kind of narrow-minded attitude is exactly what is holding back our progress as a society."

You are absolutely right. In some places there is real racism. But not here. Not now. Not you. You would never stand for that kind of limited thinking and disrespectful behavior.

☐ An Unwillingness to Educate Yourself

"How am I going to learn if people don't teach me?"

Libraries, bookstores, public television and radio programs, and the World Wide Web are all filled with useful information about race, racism, and people of all kinds. Some of these great resources can even be accessed for free. However, some renters shy away from independent learning. You may prefer to rely on the expertise of a live rental. The personal touch can be far more comforting than the sterile confines of a library, the hassles of research, or the labor of problem solving with other rentals. Some critics have considered this lazy, but renters tend to describe their need for personal instruction as a "natural human tendency."

Some renters shy away from independent learning.

Let It Rip! Easy Tear-Out Tools for Renters

These tear-out tools can make renting as fun as it is easy. Just copy or remove the tidbits below and put them right to your personal use!

Regular Renter? You should make the most of your well-earned money. Most rentals will honor this Frequent Renter card. It's a great way to forge good business relationships while you save cash!

Rent-a-Negro
FREQUENT RENTER CARD

(1)(2)(3)(4)(5)(6)(7)(8)(9)(10) **FREE!**

Ask your rental to initial this card each time you rent, and your eleventh rental is free!

© HOW TO RENT A NEGRO

Following are some quick, easy, and fun ways to recruit a rental for your event, informational needs, or just to keep you company. Feel free to copy these examples and use them in your rental pursuit.

Copy this poster and fill in your phone number. Post it in areas where you think black people will see it. Or post it in areas where you think other renters will see it. They might be able to refer you to an experienced and favorite rental.

WANTED

ARTICULATE, PERSONABLE, AND WELL-BEHAVED

BLACK PERSON
TO

- enliven social events
- answer questions about black culture
- help my life appear integrated

• WILLING TO PAY COMPETITIVE RATES •

Please Call: _ _ _ - _ _ _ _

© *HOW TO RENT A NEGRO*

You can take out an ad like the one below in your local newspaper or the local African American newspaper.

•WANTED

ARTICULATE, PERSONABLE
AND WELL-BEHAVED

•BLACK PERSON

To
Enliven Social
Events
Answer Questions
About Black Culture
And Help My Life
Appear Integrated.

WILLING TO PAY COMPETITIVE RATES.

There are plenty of ways to fill your rental needs that keep you in the driver's seat. You can put a poster in areas where you think black people will see it.

6
Quickies: Impulse Renting

Do you keep a hectic schedule? Need to rent on the fly? Developed by innovative renters, these quick-fix rentals have been used with success for years without the commitment of a more elaborate setup. It's amazing how easy it is to be a renter!

Thinking of You

It's always nice to be thought of. Only think of your black friends when something comes up about racism. It's important you tell them every time you notice racism. Surely, they don't hear enough about it in their own experience.

Don't You Need a Job?

"I'm looking for a diversity trainer for my organization. Do you do that? You must know someone who can. I can pay a small fee, not a lot. Our company has other things we have to focus on." Black people are always looking for a job and eager to educate others about black culture.

The Service Here Is Excellent!

"There was this lovely black attendant in the elevator." Next time you see a black person in formal attire, assume they are part of a service staff. Tip them if you feel generous.

You're down with the groove!

The Hip-Hop Hipster

Next time your black friend gets in your car, make sure you have some black music playing loudly on the stereo. You want to make your friend feel comfortable and show everyone that you're down with the groove.

Passive Permission

"It's OK, I can say that because my [friend/wife/lover/neighbor/maid/shoe-shine man] is black. When we're together we talk like that the whole time." It's important that the cited black person is nowhere near the scene of the quickie. Maybe the person doesn't even exist.

Fictitious Kin

Use the word "brotha" or "sista" when addressing a black person. Sometimes use a clever substitute. For example, "See you later, *Sledge!*" (a reference to Sister Sledge, a popular black singing group of actual siblings from the late 1970s). This quickie is trendy among the hipster crowd.

The Shell Game

"Really, I'm not even white, really, my skin is a more peachy-flesh-tone color. You're not black, your skin is actually brown. Anyway it's just skin. It's all the same." Skin is skin; it comes in all shades. If race is just about skin color, then just about anyone can be black, even you.

Brainy McSmarts

Having a lively intellectual discussion? Oh dear, here comes a black person. He probably won't understand what you are talking about. Better change the subject. When a black person joins the conversation make sure you drop all intelligent chitchat and make the conversation accessible.

Can't You Take a Joke?

Before you tell a prejudiced joke, make sure the black person next to you won't mind. "You're cool with this, right? I mean, it's just a joke." Racism can be lots of fun, but make sure your audience understands your sense of humor. You mean no harm. Also, remember to make fun of everybody, not just one group. Finally, if someone accuses you of being prejudiced, just remind them that stereotypes are based on truth. Everybody knows that.

My Favorite Color

The next time a black person complements you on your lovely brown sweater, return the praise with a humble rejection of its beauty. "Oh, it's sh*t brown. I don't even like it. It's such a putrid color." It's hard to not associate brown with nasty, ugly things. It's easy to forget things like chocolate, trees, the majority of people in the world, and oh, right, the skin of the person you're talking to.

"I was black in a past life."

Psychic Sympathy

"I relate to black people because I was black in a past life." Or, this renter favorite, "My skin is white, but my soul is black." Who could challenge this assertion? It's certainly hard to disprove. This mystical approach to renting has been popularized by famous renters, including Ricki Lake and Quentin Tarantino—who stylishly punctuated this move on national TV with a soulful high five.

The Invisible Man

"Black is not a color. Black is the *absence* of color. It's a scientific fact!" Renters are very attached to this concept. It seems nothing beats science for a quick way to end any argument. Keep this one handy should you need an easy way out of a discussion about racism, painting, or light theory.

Parallel Universe

"I completely relate to being black because when I was a child I had to wear glasses and everyone made fun of me." Yep. That's exactly what it's like to be black.

George of the Jungle

When discussing black people always make comparisons to animals. "She is so long and lean, just like a gazelle." Or, "He's so strong and handsome, he could be a purebred stallion." Or, a common favorite, "What a cute baby, such a sweet little monkey!"

Continual Education

"Since you're black, can you read this poem about slavery to the class?" Always call on black students to comment on anything related to or written by black people. This quickie is very popular during Black History Month. In fact, you might even ignore your black students altogether until February.

A Rose by Any Other Name

"It takes so long to say the phrase 'people of color.' Can't I just say 'colored people?' I mean the same thing. What's the difference anyway? Aren't we all some color? And what am I supposed to call you? First it was black, and then it was African American, and I'm worried that if I say the wrong thing, I'm going to be called a racist. There's so much pressure, I just can't do anything right." Language can be so confusing. Terms and phrases are cumbersome to say and difficult to remember. Just pick your favorite and stick with it.

Genocide? What Genocide?

"What is going on over there in Africa? Should we be doing something? I haven't really paid attention. What is the black community going to do about it?" Don't be concerned if thousands of black people are killed or die from disease in some remote corner of the world. There are plenty more where those came from.

The Holiday Honky

"I'd love to go to your house for the holidays. I bet your family is huge. I'm sure I'd be the only white person there. You probably eat nothing but collard greens and pigs' feet. I could be the token white person. Wouldn't that be fun?" Make sure you fill up on regular food before you go.

Everything's Relative

"I just heard about this black person on the news. Do you know him?" Yes, somewhere a long time ago, all people were related. It's true. So go ahead and ask if any two black people know each other. There's always a possibility.

Suspicious Minds

"Sir, may I search your bag?" This quickie is timely as well as timeless. Always search the bags of black people when they come through your checkpoint. When they inquire as to why you are searching their bags, assure them that the search is completely random. When the government raises suspicions about another racial group, make that group your primary search target. When that threat is over you can go back to searching the bags of black people.

Shades of Gray

"I heard you are not feeling well. Got the flu? Yeah, it's going around. I'm sorry to hear that. You do look kind of pale. Well not *pale*, 'cause you still look black. I mean, you *are* black. You can't be really pale or anything. Not like me. I'm pale. I mean, *I* can look pale. I guess you just look, well, sick. Now you look kind of nauseous. Are you going to be OK?"

Cultural Communion

"All groups endured some kind of suffering when they came to this country." When a black person talks about personal experiences of racism and discrimination, chime right in with stories about your ethnic heritage. Sure, being Swiss isn't really that different from being black.

When a black person talks about their experiences of racism and discrimination, chime right in with stories about your ethnic heritage.

The Glamorous Life

"You have to admit, there are so many great things about being black. Like I bet you never have a bad hair day." Maybe black people just need a gentle reminder of the positive things about their race, and who better to point those things out than you?

Hangin' with the Homies

(Usually used by renters in states of heightened confidence, often induced by alcohol.) During a conversation with a black person, use the words "homeboy," "homies," "nigga," "K-fresh," "J-dog," and "G-smooth." Make it clear that you are referring to a black person and yourself as if you are both homies.

Here's how to create a slang nickname: take the first initial of the person's name and add a slick descriptor like smooth or fresh:

"J-smooth," "J-fresh." If you're not that creative you can always just add the word "dawg" (dog) to someone's first initial: "J-dawg." Use with a street-sounding greeting: "Whassup, J-daawwg?!" You'll sound just like a rap star.

Let Bygones Be Bygones

"Slavery was such a long time ago. I have no idea if my relatives owned slaves. And it wouldn't make any difference if they did. You and I are equal now. All that bad stuff is just history." Over the course of history, renters have tried to bury the past as best they can. The trouble is, everywhere they dig they keep uncovering sacred Native American burial grounds.

Med School

"This medication hasn't really been tested on black people. Let's see how you do with it." The medical establishment hasn't done nearly enough research on black health, so you might as well experiment.

Guilty Until . . . Guilty

"What do you call a black person in a courtroom in a three-piece suit? The defendant." Are you a lawyer, judge, or reporter? You can rent as you work. Do your best to incriminate, interrogate, and incarcerate as many black people as the prisons can hold.

The Great Political Melting Pot

"And now, someone who embodies the potential of America." Whoops, did you plan a political gathering without a minority representative? Quick, try to find someone who has "pulled themselves up by their own bootstraps" and will use that phrase in a speech. You could write the speech for them. Make sure to include popular phrases such as "all men are created equal," "the American dream," "the land of opportunity," "the melting pot," and "only in America." Make sure the speaker avoids phrases like "preferential treatment," "glass ceiling," "white supremacy," and "racial barriers."

Follow the N . . . Leader

"Keep an eye on that person. He looks suspicious." This classic quickie is popular with sales people in stores of all kinds. Some may even call it "instinctual." Follow any black person that comes into your store or business. Ask immediately if he needs help or what *exactly* he is looking for. Keep him in your sight (and within your grasp) from the moment he enters until he leaves. After all, you're just being helpful. If he purchases something, make sure you test his cash to make sure it's real.

Affirmative Reaction

"I bet you got this job because you are black. That's what happened to my cousin. This black girl and she applied for the same job and the black girl got it. It was because of affirmative action. Black people get things handed to them." Don't be shy. Go ahead and remind your rental of all the ways the system is slanted to help black people, and the many, many ways that white people are mistreated as a result.

Boogie On

"Hey, can you teach me how to dance? I have no sense of natural rhythm. I'm so white. But I bet you're a great dancer. Maybe you can come over and teach me and my friends." After hearing some black people complain that white people have no rhythm, innovative renters came up with this controversial experiment. The world is still waiting for the results.

Flattery Gets You Nowhere

"Black people are all so beautiful. You have such pretty skin, wild hair, those big lips, and the whitest teeth! Every black person I've ever seen has the brightest white teeth." Though it's been done, try to avoid using this quickie if the black person is complaining about their incoming wisdom teeth. They're probably in enough pain as it is.

"I bet you're a great dancer. Can you come over and teach me and my friends?"

Imitation of Life

When you talk to a black person, use your best put-on street accent. Use as many slang words as you can, even if you don't know what they mean. Try using "black English" by mixing up your verb tenses, using wrong subject-verb agreement, and slurring your words. Ain't that how real black peoples talks?

Rosy Cheeks

"That was so embarrassing for you. But wow, I can't tell if you're blushing. That's so cool. You don't blush, do you? I mean, if you blushed, no one could tell. That's great. You are so lucky. It must be great to be you. Ooh. Now I'm blushing, I guess you can see that."

Make It Go Away!

"I don't see race. I don't think of you as black. I don't think of myself as any race. I just see people as people. The most important race is the human race." Some renters like to focus on the big picture. Race can be so divisive. There are so many labels separating us when we are members of the same group. It's awful. Who came up with all these categories anyway?

Silence Is Deadly

Whenever you see one of these techniques being implemented, stand by and watch. Don't interfere. Don't speak up. Don't interrupt the renter. Simply observe. When the renter leaves, whisper a quick apology to the black person and change the subject.

FEE: $250 per quickie
    ($15,000 if used on a nationally televised program)

Don't Shoot! It's Only a Rental:
A Special Segment for
Law Enforcement Officers

Throughout history, officers of the law have been a frequent and reliable group of renters. Police officers, sheriffs, state troopers, and security guards are a staple of every rental's daily encounters. Law enforcement officers have come to depend on regular rentals as part of daily work. Those of you employed as brave defenders of the law have worked hard to cement this deep historical bond.

The fine-tuning of this long-term relationship has been the center of much debate. Renting protocol has been a discussion in police precincts for generations. As both sides seek a compromise, rentals have also investigated how best to respond to the needs of police officers and have come to understand that they require special attention. Requests from police officers who want to harass, arrest, beat, stun, or shoot black people are quite common. As you know, police officers often request a drop-in appearance, based on a minor traffic violation (some of your favorites might be failure to use a turn signal, failure to wear a seatbelt, or failure to fix a broken taillight). Once you stop a prospective rental for such a violation, you can complete your transaction on the street during a work shift, conveniently collecting your own pay while you rent.

Unfortunately, many police requests are difficult for rentals to fulfill. Police-rental interaction can be very exciting. In the heat of the moment it may be difficult to keep in mind that the black person in front of you was not purchased outright. Remember, that is illegal. Since the black person is only a rental, he must be returned intact, undamaged, and in his original condition.[1] As a way of keeping this in mind during your shift, perhaps you can practice chanting under your breath the gentle reminder, "Don't shoot. It's only a rental."

1. This reminder also applies to teachers, lawyers, judges, psychotherapists, doctors, and members of the armed forces. Please make every effort to see that your rentals are returned free from damage and wear and tear.

You can practice chanting under your breath the gentle reminder, "Don't shoot. It's only a rental."

These interactions have affected the economics of renting. Most renters do not provide for the possibility of permanent damage: loss of property, mobility, or life. The cost of repairs for even temporary damage can drive rental fees through the roof, and permanent damage cannot be adequately addressed by financial compensation. Since many courts do not penalize officers of the law for this particular breach of contract, it can be difficult for rentals to recoup the out-of-pocket costs that often accompany police interaction.

Police requests have also had an impact on the reputation of many rentals. Renters have been complaining that their rentals often arrive late, shaken, or injured due to interaction with police. Rentals' family members are beginning to grumble, "When you go to work I never know if you're going to come home." Repeated absences have significantly damaged the hard-earned reputations of reliable rentals. Many rentals are opting to add extra time to their travel hours to account for police encounters. In any good business, time is money. These difficulties are causing an increase in rental fees worldwide.

In addition, because many police rentals are spontaneous or "impulse rentals," it can be difficult to plan around them. Basic impulse rentals or quickies usually take a few minutes—or sometimes only seconds. Police impulse rentals, which may involve bodily injury, detainment, or termination of life, take quite a while longer. Again, these demands make the business unpredictable, inconvenience rentals and renters, and damage the credibility of the market. When possible, prearrange your rental instead of acting on impulse. This way, all parties can be aware and in agreement about the course and duration of the rental activities. If you have been given permission to injure or take the life of your rental, please keep a copy of your invoice on hand as documentation to that effect.

On the whole, rentals are committed to the ideas of citizenship and country and thus want to support officers of the law in any way possible. After all, you are the same officers who keep the streets and cities safe.

Do You Want Fries with That Negro?

Sample Rental Applications

What does a rental application look like? How do I write a rental request? Do I have to fulfill every request? Whether you're a renter or a rental, the examples below will help answer your questions and give you a sense of the demands, desires, and creative spirit of both groups.

These examples show renters how you can tailor your requests to fill your specific requirements down to the smallest details. Curious about what kinds of services you can request? You'll see that renters are not shy about their needs. These examples will help you to craft a request that grabs the attention of a rental.

These examples give rentals a sense of what types of renters are right for you. Are there situations in which your talents shine? Are there certain requests you'd rather turn away? You need to establish your own specialties and limitations. You might become an expert at handling racist family members, but be less enthusiastic about attending corporate gatherings. Knowing the range of potential requests will give you an advantage in deciding what kind of jobs to accept.

As you review the requests below, ask yourself, is this the kind of experience you're looking for, or is this particular scenario best fulfilled by someone else? How much would you pay for these services as a renter? As a rental, how much would you charge to fulfill these requests? Use the check boxes below each rental to record your response.

These are actual requests received at rent-a-negro.com. Names and some details have been changed to maintain confidentiality.

NAME: Christopher Thomas

EVENT TYPE: Private/personal gathering

NUMBER OF PEOPLE AT EVENT: 80

LOCATION: Rochester, Minnesota

DESCRIPTION: It's a dinner party and I really want it to be diverse.

HAVE YOU USED BLACK PEOPLE BEFORE? No

DESCRIBE YOUR PREVIOUS EXPERIENCE WITH BLACK PEOPLE: I have never met a black person. I don't know what to say.

TELL US ABOUT YOURSELF: I don't know any black people, I want my life to be more diverse. Please help me find one.

☐ Perfect! Where do I sign up? ☐ I have a few questions
☐ Not quite my type ☐ I would pay/charge: $_____

NAME: Craig Stephens

NUMBER OF PEOPLE AT EVENT: 50

LOCATION: Idaho

DESCRIPTION: Just a graduation party. There will be a keg. And music. Just a good time. The rental would be just to give the party atmosphere.

TELL US ABOUT YOURSELF: Um. I'm having a graduation party this coming Sunday, and I don't have any black friends. I want black friends, but Idaho is so backwards and out of the loop. I do have a hip-hop show on my college radio station, so I'm trying. So anyway, I was wondering if I could rent a negro for my graduation party. It would be so swell. Thanks.

☐ Perfect! Where do I sign up? ☐ I have a few questions
☐ Not quite my type ☐ I would pay/charge: $_____

NAME: Miranda Moore

EVENT TYPE: Private/personal gathering

NUMBER OF PEOPLE AT EVENT: 3

LOCATION: Toronto, Ontario, Canada,

DESCRIPTION: It's just a little get together with some friends.

TELL US ABOUT YOURSELF: I'm curious about African culture and wish to impress my friends with my knowledge and diversity. I am very outgoing and love people, but I can't seem to get along with my black roommate here in college. We live in the same 4 bedroom apt. There weren't enough people to fill our apt. so they put her in the apt. with us. I realize that I have never really had to associate with black people, but now I am being forced to. But I just want to see if I can rent a person to be a friend of mine from high school and maybe she will think that she relates to me more and that I can relate to her. And too, maybe I can really learn something in the process about black people.

OTHER SERVICES: Maybe some hair touching and questions. Come by the apartment and eat lunch and watch TV, so that she can see me with them.

☐ Perfect! Where do I sign up? ☐ I have a few questions
☐ Not quite my type ☐ I would pay/charge: $_____

NAME: Effie Harris

EVENT TYPE: Corporate/business gathering

NUMBER OF PEOPLE AT EVENT: 12

DESCRIPTION: I have an upcoming meeting with the urban division of our sales and marketing department. I think the pitch would fly a little better with a negro on my side agreeing with my views.

HOW MANY BLACK PEOPLE DO YOU KNOW? 4

DESCRIBE YOUR PREVIOUS EXPERIENCE WITH BLACK PEOPLE: They don't seem to understand me

TELL US ABOUT YOURSELF: I am a white man looking for a black person to enhance my business connections.

OTHER SERVICES: Need business attire (do they come with that) and vocabulary consisting of 4 or more sylabol words. Also, fluent in ebonics

☐ Perfect! Where do I sign up? ☐ I have a few questions
☐ Not quite my type ☐ I would pay/charge: $_____

NAME: Robert Woodson

EVENT TYPE: Corporate/business gathering

NUMBER OF PEOPLE AT EVENT: 50

LOCATION: Country club

DESCRIPTION: Annual business dinner party

HAVE YOU USED BLACK PEOPLE BEFORE? Yes

DID YOU PAY? I did not pay

HOW MANY BLACK PEOPLE DO YOU KNOW? 4

DESCRIBE YOUR PREVIOUS EXPERIENCE WITH BLACK PEOPLE: Depending upon where you find them, they can either be loud and boisterous or just like any other person.

TELL US ABOUT YOURSELF: I am a white man looking for a black person to enhance my business connections.

OTHER SERVICES: High Question Volume

☐ Perfect! Where do I sign up?　☐ I have a few questions
☐ Not quite my type　☐ I would pay/charge: $_____

NAME: Alex Dumont

EVENT TYPE: Ongoing/retainer

NUMBER OF PEOPLE AT EVENT: 1

LOCATION: Memphis, Tennessee

DESCRIPTION: educational

HAVE YOU USED BLACK PEOPLE BEFORE? No

TELL US ABOUT YOURSELF: My name is Alex. I'm a single white male, almost twenty seven years of age. It seems about time that I meet a negro. It's weird that I've never seen one, growing up in the urban south, but Memphis, Tennessee can be so divided I've heard. Please send me a negro ASAP so that I may too enjoy the American melting pot experience.

Thank you in advance for your response.

Also, do you have any financial assistance/scholarships available?

☐ Perfect! Where do I sign up?　☐ I have a few questions
☐ Not quite my type　　　　　　☐ I would pay/charge: $_____

NAME: Jannine George

EVENT TYPE: Private/personal gathering

NUMBER OF PEOPLE AT EVENT: 30

LOCATION: Austin, Texas

DESCRIPTION: A social function, My family adopted a new black baby.

HAVE YOU USED BLACK PEOPLE BEFORE? No

HOW MANY BLACK PEOPLE DO YOU KNOW? 7

☐ Perfect! Where do I sign up?　☐ I have a few questions
☐ Not quite my type　　　　　　☐ I would pay/charge: $_____

NAME: Jeannie Brock

EVENT TYPE: Private/personal gathering

NUMBER OF PEOPLE AT EVENT: 200

LOCATION: Augusta, Georgia

DESCRIPTION: It is an arts and culture festival being held at a local ballroom center here in the area. There will be plenty of mingling and networking opportunities available.

HAVE YOU USED BLACK PEOPLE BEFORE? Yes

DID YOU PAY? I paid

DESCRIBE YOUR PREVIOUS EXPERIENCE WITH BLACK PEOPLE: It really depends on the social situation and the mood in which they are in.

TELL US ABOUT YOURSELF: I think the concept is long overdue. I am interested to see if these kind of services are actually available for political functions.

❏ Perfect! Where do I sign up? ❏ I have a few questions
❏ Not quite my type ❏ I would pay/charge: $_____

NAME: Frank O'Mally

EVENT TYPE: Private/personal gathering

NUMBER OF PEOPLE AT EVENT: 38

LOCATION: Anywhere will do

DESCRIPTION: Lynching

HAVE YOU USED BLACK PEOPLE BEFORE? Yes

DID YOU PAY? I did not pay

HOW MANY BLACK PEOPLE DO YOU KNOW? 4

DESCRIBE YOUR PREVIOUS EXPERIENCE WITH BLACK PEOPLE: They sure do plead and twitch when you hoist them up on the branch.

TELL US ABOUT YOURSELF: Well, I have been "interacting" with negroes for quite some time. I'm hooked!

OTHER SERVICES: Three feet of environmentally-friendly hemp rope

❏ Perfect! Where do I sign up? ❏ I have a few questions
❏ Not quite my type ❏ I would pay/charge: $_____

NAME: Amy Mills

EVENT TYPE: Individual

NUMBER OF PEOPLE AT EVENT: 6

LOCATION: Des Moines, IA

DESCRIPTION: Just a family gathering to meet my daughter's fiancé.

HOW MANY BLACK PEOPLE DO YOU KNOW? 3

DESCRIBE YOUR PREVIOUS EXPERIENCE WITH BLACK PEOPLE: Positive.

TELL US ABOUT YOURSELF: I need a black companion to make my daughter's black fiancé feel more comfortable when I meet him.

OTHER SERVICES: 3–4 hair grabs

☐ Perfect! Where do I sign up? ☐ I have a few questions
☐ Not quite my type ☐ I would pay/charge: $_____

NAME: Gloria Roberts

EVENT TYPE: Private/personal gathering

NUMBER OF PEOPLE AT EVENT: 12

LOCATION: Aberdeen South Dakota

DESCRIPTION: Bridge group

HAVE YOU USED BLACK PEOPLE BEFORE? No

HOW MANY BLACK PEOPLE DO YOU KNOW? Lots

DESCRIBE YOUR PREVIOUS EXPERIENCE WITH BLACK PEOPLE: I love black people, they are almost as good as white people!

TELL US ABOUT YOURSELF: I am 65, and most of my friends don't believe that I love black people, so I want to prove them wrong.

OTHER SERVICES: Hair Touching, Racist Guests

☐ Perfect! Where do I sign up? ☐ I have a few questions
☐ Not quite my type ☐ I would pay/charge: $_____

NAME: William Carson

EVENT TYPE: Corporate/business meeting

NUMBER OF PEOPLE AT EVENT: 20

LOCATION: Cambridge, Ontario, Canada

DESCRIPTION: A work party, with a open bar, lots of single ladies will be there.

HAVE YOU USED BLACK PEOPLE BEFORE? No

DESCRIBE YOUR PREVIOUS EXPERIENCE WITH BLACK PEOPLE:
I found them to be very polite people

TELL US ABOUT YOURSELF: Well, I am a shy guy, and I think having a negro come with me to the bar will help me attract the ladies.

☐ Perfect! Where do I sign up? ☐ I have a few questions
☐ Not quite my type ☐ I would pay/charge: $_____

NAME: Paul Strayer

EVENT TYPE: Private/personal gathering

NUMBER OF PEOPLE AT EVENT: 150

LOCATION: Fond Du Lac, Wisconsin

OTHER SERVICES: lots of touching (i.e.-punching and kicking)

HAVE YOU USED BLACK PEOPLE BEFORE? Yes

DID YOU PAY? I did not pay

HOW MANY BLACK PEOPLE DO YOU KNOW? Lots

DESCRIBE YOUR PREVIOUS EXPERIENCE WITH BLACK PEOPLE:
I always end up with a smile after they stop moving.

☐ Perfect! Where do I sign up? ☐ I have a few questions
☐ Not quite my type ☐ I would pay/charge: $_____

NAME: Rick Taylor

EVENT TYPE: Drop-in Appearance

NUMBER OF PEOPLE AT EVENT: 25

LOCATION: Houston, Texas

DESCRIPTION: I need to convince everybody in the newsroom I'm down with it.

HAVE YOU USED BLACK PEOPLE BEFORE? Yes

DID YOU PAY? I did not pay

HOW MANY BLACK PEOPLE DO YOU KNOW? 10

DESCRIBE YOUR PREVIOUS EXPERIENCE WITH BLACK PEOPLE:
Half my superiors and most of the editors are black.

TELL US ABUT YOURSELF: Heard about jungle fever . . . wanted to experience it first hand!

OTHER SERVICES: High Question Volume, 10 Hair Touches

HOW DID YOU HEAR ABOUT RENT-A-NEGRO? Who doesn't know about rent-a-negro?

❏ Perfect! Where do I sign up?   ❏ I have a few questions
❏ Not quite my type   ❏ I would pay/charge: $_____

☐ Perfect! Where do I sign up? ☐ I have a few questions
☐ Not quite my type ☐ I would pay/charge: $_____

NAME: Simon Gray

EVENT TYPE: Corporate/business meeting

NUMBER OF PEOPLE AT EVENT: 30

LOCATION: Los Angeles, California

DESCRIPTION: Diversity meeting

DESCRIBE YOUR PREVIOUS EXPERIENCE WITH BLACK PEOPLE: No comment, I'm still processing the experience. I'm seeing a therapist about it and am not ready to talk about it.

TELL US ABOUT YOURSELF: You are the only service that I've found. I'm the multicultural director at my company and I need a spokesperson to be on my team, a black woman preferably, to help me show the black people at my company that I can relate to them.

OTHER SERVICES: Black testimonials (e.g. What is it like to be black)

☐ Perfect! Where do I sign up? ☐ I have a few questions
☐ Not quite my type ☐ I would pay/charge: $_____

NAME: Janice Doughtry

EVENT TYPE: Individual

NUMBER OF PEOPLE AT EVENT: 1

LOCATION: Chicago, Illinois

DESCRIPTION: Party

HAVE YOU USED BLACK PEOPLE BEFORE? Yes

DID YOU PAY? I paid

HOW MANY BLACK PEOPLE DO YOU KNOW? 100

DESCRIBE YOUR PREVIOUS EXPERIENCE WITH BLACK PEOPLE: Black people are great people.

TELL US ABOUT YOURSELF: I want to know what it is like to hang out with a black person.

☐ Perfect! Where do I sign up? ☐ I have a few questions
☐ Not quite my type ☐ I would pay/charge: $_____

NAME: Helen Carlente

EVENT TYPE: Nonprofit function

NUMBER OF PEOPLE AT EVENT: Unknown

LOCATION: East Orange, New Jersey

DESCRIPTION: A ribbon-cutting event .

HAVE YOU USED BLACK PEOPLE BEFORE? No

HOW MANY BLACK PEOPLE DO YOU KNOW? 3

DESCRIBE YOUR PREVIOUS EXPERIENCE WITH BLACK PEOPLE: Primarily pleasant but distant.

TELL US ABOUT YOURSELF: I am a land survey engineer with the county. I work in an urban setting and am attending the ribbon-cutting ceremony for the launch of a new community development center. I would prefer to have someone who appears, at least on the surface, familiar with environmental issues and the attendees.

❏ Perfect! Where do I sign up?   ❏ I have a few questions
❏ Not quite my type   ❏ I would pay/charge: $_____

NAME: Amanda Nelson

EVENT TYPE: Private/personal gathering

NUMBER OF PEOPLE AT EVENT: 10

LOCATION: Hillsborough New Jersey

DESCRIPTION: I've invited a bunch of people I know for a party at my house so they could see that I'm friends with a black person.

HAVE YOU USED BLACK PEOPLE BEFORE? No

HOW MANY BLACK PEOPLE DO YOU KNOW? 2

DESCRIBE YOUR PREVIOUS EXPERIENCE WITH BLACK PEOPLE: She hated me because I was white.

TELL US ABOUT YOURSELF: I am very white and there are rumors going around that I hate black people, I get beat up a lot because of them. I want to rent a black person so I could show them I'm not racist.

OTHER SERVICES: Call Her Sista, Dance Lessons

❏ Perfect! Where do I sign up?   ❏ I have a few questions
❏ Not quite my type   ❏ I would pay/charge: $_____

NAME: Marcia Swanson

EVENT TYPE: Private/personal gathering

NUMBER OF PEOPLE AT EVENT: 15

LOCATION: New York, New York

DESCRIPTION: Poets and artists at a gallery opening.

HAVE YOU USED BLACK PEOPLE BEFORE? Yes

DID YOU PAY? I paid

HOW MANY BLACK PEOPLE DO YOU KNOW? 1051

DESCRIBE YOUR PREVIOUS EXPERIENCE WITH BLACK PEOPLE: Childhood friends and enemies, Africans living abroad in Europe, people in my Harlem neighborhood.

TELL US ABOUT YOURSELF: I am seeking cool companionship that will reflect my compassionate integrationist attitudes.

OTHER SERVICES: High Question and Smile volume

☐ Perfect! Where do I sign up? ☐ I have a few questions
☐ Not quite my type ☐ I would pay/charge: $_____

So You Want to Be a Rental?

Getting Over That Helpless Feeling

It finally happens. There you are, just like every other Thursday, having lunch with the usual group—friends, colleagues, and local gossips. You share opinions on politics and people. You exchange the standard complaints about the weather and the boredom of work. You admire your ability to withstand it all with a winning smile and a stylish suit. Everything seems perfectly normal, a relaxed routine. Then, as you put down your sparkling water and pick up your cappuccino, one of your lunch mates turns to you and asks that pivotal question, "Hey, how do you think black people are going to vote in the upcoming election? My office is working on an ad campaign and we need to know what you think of the candidates."

You pause for a moment, contemplating the question. As you begin to respond, you can't quite place your mixed feelings about this exchange. You stop, this time fully frozen at the thought. "This can't be true. Have I become the official black expert among my peers?" You search through the rules of etiquette in your mind. "No, she wouldn't really . . . well, it's not the first time. Last week someone asked me to a party just to shake things up. Is this becoming a pattern?" You think of your parents and friends. "I wonder if other black people find themselves in these same kinds of situations? There must be a way to capitalize on this and be paid for the time I spend being black on demand."

You ponder hopefully and almost concede defeat when you realize you haven't been charging for a lifetime of billable hours. You take a deep breath. "How did this happen?" you ask yourself. Has it always been this way and you've just awoken to the reality? How could you be so out of touch, so behind the times? You've heard all the talk about diversity and multiculturalism and you pride yourself on being in sync with current trends. How did this opportunity pass you by? That popular television show used to be all white, and now there's a black character on it. The latest fashion ideas are always on that show, and now you wonder if you're a trendy accessory.

You are reluctant to bring your realizations up with your white cohorts. This is understandable, and a very common reaction. You don't know what your friends would think if you presented them with a bill in response to an innocent question or a kind invitation to a social gathering. On the other hand, they are certainly benefiting from your presence. They didn't ask your other lunch companion about how the Irish were voting this year.

Are you the only one doing this work for free? You certainly aren't going to point that out. But how can you change the situation? You say to yourself, "There must be an invoice for this kind of thing. After all, aren't most specialists paid for their services? My friend is a consultant—this must be right up her alley."

Imagine this: you reach into your briefcase and pull out a convenient invoice and say, "I'd be happy to give you my opinion as a black person. Just fill out this form." After checking the appropriate boxes and signing the invoice, your friend gives you a check for a $75. You shake hands and offer your official black opinion on the subject in question. "Thanks," she replies, and you both order dessert.

Now wouldn't that be something?

It's clear that demand for certified rent-a-negroes is high. There's no doubt that you are qualified to do the job. You've been volunteering your services for years. Why not start charging fees? Would a dentist, teacher, or hairdresser give away every session for free? Of course not. You should be appropriately compensated for the service you provide your community. Sure, you may decide to do some pro bono work. Philanthropy is good for the soul. It makes you feel good to donate some of your time, but by no means should you give away your expertise to anyone who asks. Time is money, and information is a valued commodity. When was the last time an electrician came to your house and didn't charge you? Would you ask the caterer to show up with food for your party and leave without being paid? If you were a plumber you might answer a question or two for free. But if you're going to travel to someone's home and spend time covered in sludge while you clear out an unruly clog, you would certainly present them with a bill when you leave.

You're not alone in your entrepreneurial spirit. Rent-a-negro.com receives countless requests from qualified rentals, inquiring about working for the service. Here are a few e-mails from would-be rentals around the world:

> "I think this service is great. I live in the whitest state I've ever known. I have little kids that come up to me and rub my skin as if the blackness is going to come off. And that's on a good day!"

> "I visited your rent-a-negro Web site! What a fabulous idea! I am an African American woman, graduate of a prestigious University, and I would love to work with you over the summer. Are you hiring or looking for individuals who are willing to rent themselves out? I'll e-mail you a copy of my résumé if you are."

> "How do I become involved? I want to be rented. I live in a famously racist city and would love to show the world that not all blacks fit into the mold. I speak perfect English, am very knowledgeable on a wide range of subjects, present a professional appearance, and exhibit grace under fire."

> "Through high school, college and into my years in business I have been amazed at the degree to which much of America's white citizenry has managed to so effectively isolate themselves. My experience has been very positive when exposed to these individuals. They come to realize that we are people too, with hopes, dreams, aspirations, fears, and frustrations. Think of how much more comfortable the world would be if we could get white people to relax."

"Are there any job openings left at rent-a-negro? I possess a smarmy, dry-witted approach that disarms most white people that are invasively curious or have low social, educational, or stereotypical expectations in their interactions with people of color. Or those whites that feel compelled to make me the spokes-negro. My smug yet erudite responses to asinine questions and comments will have your customers coming back for more. I play the role of the sophisticated 'Sapphire' very well."

"It would be about time I got paid for what I do on a daily basis. In my line of business, I legitimize white people all the time."

"[I would make a good rent-a-negro because] I was raised in the affluent, white-bread-belt of Southern California. I am comfortable and confident being the only black person in a social setting or the corporate boardroom. I am educated, articulate, and personable. I can differentiate between escargot, salad, and dinner forks. Rock is my favorite type of music, I love sushi and I drive a Volvo."

There's no need to send in your résumé. You've already been hired plenty of times. How often have you heard yourself say, "If only I had a dime for every time someone asked me what the black community thinks of Jesse Jackson, Michael Jackson, or Mike Tyson"? Well here's your chance to collect those dimes and more.

How Can I Tell If I'm Being Rented? A Quiz

Chances are, you might already be a rent-a-negro. Before you start collecting fees or advertising your services, take this simple diagnostic quiz. These are just some of the many services that rentals fill on a daily basis. If you are filling these same services, it may be time to write up a few bills.

Check all the boxes that apply. The score for each box is listed. If any of these events happen to you more than once a day, give yourself ten points. You've earned it.

	Daily	Weekly	Monthly	Holidays/ Black History Month	Once a Year
Frequency:					
Points:	5	4	3	2	1
You are the only black person in the room.	☐	☐	☐	☐	☐
When people say "African American," they point at you.	☐	☐	☐	☐	☐
When you enter a room, racism suddenly becomes a conversational topic.	☐	☐	☐	☐	☐
People are eager to tell you about the black person they just met.	☐	☐	☐	☐	☐
You are told, "You are so articulate."	☐	☐	☐	☐	☐
You are asked to speak for all black people.	☐	☐	☐	☐	☐
You are asked to validate or disprove racial stereotypes.	☐	☐	☐	☐	☐
You are referred to as "an exception," or you hear the phrase "you're different."	☐	☐	☐	☐	☐

	Frequency: Daily	Weekly	Monthly	Holidays/ Black History Month	Once a Year
Points:	**5**	**4**	**3**	**2**	**1**
People ask you how to recruit other black people for their organizations.	☐	☐	☐	☐	☐
People ask you for your fried chicken recipe.	☐	☐	☐	☐	☐
You are picked first in a basketball pickup game.	☐	☐	☐	☐	☐
People add syllables to your name. (Your name is Marc, but they call you Marcus).*	☐	☐	☐	☐	☐
People ask you to obtain drugs for them.	☐	☐	☐	☐	☐
People make up slang words around you.	☐	☐	☐	☐	☐
Your invitations to events increase during the month of February.	☐	☐	☐	☐	☐
People ask you to explain rap music.	☐	☐	☐	☐	☐
You hear the phrase "people like you."	☐	☐	☐	☐	☐
People ask you about the financial aid, scholarship, affirmative action, or charity that has helped you "come so far."	☐	☐	☐	☐	☐
People show delight when you use words that rhyme.	☐	☐	☐	☐	☐
For actors: you are asked to play the role of the maid, driver, criminal, prostitute, pimp, or drug addict. For nonactors: people assume that you or one of your relatives has been or is currently employed in one of the above roles.	☐	☐	☐	☐	☐
You are asked, "Why can you use the *n*-word and I can't?"	☐	☐	☐	☐	☐

* Or as is frequently the case for the author of this book, your name is damali but people call you "damalia."

If you scored above five points on this quiz, you are spending a good portion of time as a rent-a-negro. It's time to collect the debt society owes you. If you scored above seventy-five points on this quiz, it is highly recommended that you look into a therapeutic retreat to lower your stress and risk for potential stress-related illnesses.

Now you can begin to charge for the services you provide your neighbors, friends, colleagues, even the random stranger at the bus stop. Providing work for free is exhausting, especially if you already work another job. No wonder you have days when you feel tired, bitter, angry, sad, tense, or like you just want to run away from the world. Ever think, "If one more white person asks me about being black I'm going to explode?" Well, now you don't have to feel like exploding. Once you start getting paid, you may even look forward to the next question coming your way.

Note: you may only be a rental for a certain group of people or for certain times of the year. Perhaps rental activity in your life increases around Christmas, Black History Month, or the NBA finals? Sure, it happens to every rental. Whatever your circumstance, daily or special-occasion rental, you can find a way to get compensated for your work.

# Frequently Asked Questions (FAQ)

How do I become a rent-a-negro?

Most black people are already active rentals and have been for years. It's not as hard as you might think to offer your services to any Joe, Pam, or Charlie in your community. Make a list of the people you've already worked for. Your first step may be to issue a series of retroactive bills. Don't worry about upsetting these relationships. You and your friends have always compensated each other for the help provided each other. Remember last month when your neighbor fixed your showerhead? You took him out to dinner the next week. Have confidence that your friends and acquaintances will be delighted to pay you for your years of work. Then you can ask them if they are interested in hiring you again. Any successful business nurtures existing relationships. Perhaps you can offer a repeat-renter discount. This discount will help build customer loyalty, a cornerstone of any successful venture. Once you build a strong business as a rental, you may even be able to retire from your other job.

How much should I charge?

Rental services should be both practical and affordable, priced per hour and type. You can refer to the fee schedule in chapter 5 as a guideline for pricing your services. Remember that you are an expert in your field and your rates should reflect this expertise. If you have special skills, feel free to add those to your invoice. Perhaps you can translate "black English" or cook great sweet potato pie. You can charge extra any time these skills are required. Remember to keep a running tab during any rental event. Little renter impulses can add up and result in large earnings for you!

How does billing work?

When you arrange a rental, present your renter with an invoice that details the agreed services and a fee estimate. You may want to ask for half of the total fee prior to the event as a deposit. Decide ahead of time if you can accept personal checks or credit cards in lieu of cash. Often renters act on impulse. In case of this, you should carry ready-made invoices on you at all times. You might want to make invoices that list standard fees for hair grabs, skin color comparisons, and black opinions. These are all common renter quickies. Make sure the invoice lists an address (a post office box) where the renter can send payment. Don't hesitate, quickies are fast encounters. When someone reaches for your hair, you reach for an invoice!

What is retroactive billing?

Whoops, did you forget to issue an invoice for the last time someone rubbed your soft skin? That's $75 you missed collecting. That friend who needed your black opinion last week also owes you $75. Did someone ask you to be his or her date (and the only black person) at the office holiday party? That could tally over $500. Just tally what they owe and lay it on 'em. As an incentive many rentals offer a reduced rate to people who tally their own past-due bill.

What can I expect once I am rented?

After signing a rental invoice, your renter will make any needed arrangements with you. When you arrive as a rental, collect the rest of your fees and then simply interact according to the expectations outlined in the contract. You might not be able to be yourself, but try to enjoy yourself.

Is confidentiality important?

Yes. Renters can be a very private bunch. The safer they feel with you as a rental, the more business you will generate. It's important that no one know that you are a rental except you and your renter. Through history, black people have gained a wealth of experience protecting the privacy of renters. Keeping a renter's confidence is key to building a long-standing relationship with a dependable income source. It also allows renters to interact freely at events knowing you'll follow your contract instructions to the letter. You'll be proud to see how comfortable and enthusiastic they are about your work.

Who can be a rent-a-negro?

Just about anyone! The doctor you saw last week went to medical school for only a few years. You've been doing this for a lifetime. Have confidence in your qualifications. Renters have been confident in their rentals for centuries.

Walk This Way:
Becoming a Successful Rental

Before you become an official rent-a-negro, there are a few things you'll need to consider. Becoming a successful rental means striking a delicate balance between a renter's expectation and your own style. Renters want their rentals to represent the latest in black image and sophistication. But they don't want to lose the shock value that accompanies the unexpected presence of a black person in their midst. As you read earlier, one aspiring rental wrote, "I am educated, articulate, and personable. I can differentiate between escargot, salad, and dinner forks. . . . I love sushi and I drive a Volvo." You may have all those things, but can you throw down about ballin' on the weekends? You might have majored in English literature, but can you twitch your head just so while you "talk black"? You may have a love for specialty liquors, but brush up on drinking forties out of paper bags. You never know what might come in handy.

Here are a few pointers to help you navigate some of the trickier subjects and issues that accompany rental events. Each one will assist you in becoming a successful and happy rent-a-negro.

Enjoy Being Black

OK, so being black isn't always a piece of double-decker chocolate cake, but your renter didn't hire you to listen to your frustrations. In order to thrive in this business, you should help your customers feel not only that you are an expert in your field but that you take great pride in the service you provide. This is a delicate balance. Show enthusiasm with moderation. You're not at a black power rally, you're

If any discussion about the subject of race is to start, let the renters or their guests bring it up. Don't worry, they know you're black.

on a job. Remember that mechanic who changed your oil last year? He spent the whole time nagging you about taking better care of your car. You haven't been back to see him since. Don't make this same mistake as a rental. You want to keep your renters coming back for more.

Don't Play the Race Card

You *are* the race card. You can relax and enjoy being black without drawing any extra attention to that fact. People on the other side of the room who catch a glimpse of your dark figure drifting from the punch bowl to the buffet table will start talking about race. They will talk about race when you excuse yourself to the bathroom. They will politely turn down the whitefish appetizers and stammer when they answer that they take their after-dinner coffee "bl-black." Guests will chat to each other for weeks to come, "Did you get a chance to talk to that interesting black person?" They'll brag that they spent a whole half hour chatting with you while their friend only spent ten minutes. If any discussion about the subject of race is to start, let the renters or their guests bring it up. Don't worry, they know you're black.

Dress for Success

What you wear to your rental event can be as important as what you say. Clothing and hairstyle speak volumes, and you don't want your style to drown out the entertaining conversational banter that makes you so rentable. Let your clothing support your image. You want to come across as unique yet approachable. It's the classic rental's paradox: how do I stand out and fit in simultaneously? First off, be very specific in your rental contract. Ask your renter to describe in detail the expected attire for the event. They might say to you, "Just wear whatever you want. I want you to feel comfortable." Often this is a subtle test. Will you show up in a sweats and sneakers to attend the opera? Wouldn't that be a hoot! Don't fall for this common ploy. Get the dress details before you arrive.

Once you have the clothing parameters, fulfill them with neutral mainstream clothes. Look *your* best without looking *the* best. You don't want to upstage your host or anyone else at the event. Avoid anything with Afrocentric or ethnic flair. Remember, your skin is black enough. Your outfit doesn't have to come from the motherland. Wear affordable rather than expensive designers. Renters want to give you a peek into their world. If you are already wearing their favorite designer, they may think you're a regular visitor. Save the high fashion for when you're with friends.

STYLISH TIP

Don't make this common clothing faux pas. No matter how casual the event, don't wear the latest in urban gear. Many renters voice a puzzling but consistent apprehension with regard to urban fashion. "Those people who wear baggy pants," has become code for "future criminal." You don't want to instill fear in your renter, at least not as a result of your clothing. For everyone's benefit, it's best to leave the hip-hop style back at the crib.

Hair is a major focal point of any rental experience. So many renters who have become career clients started out by touching the hair of a black person. Many were just children when their small pale fingers first reached for the hair of a black classmate. The hair grab's rich historical foundation was laid years ago when white people routinely touched the hair of an enslaved black person for good luck. Now it's a classic first-time rental. For centuries, your hair has been a central part of their intercultural experience. It's recommended that you keep your hair natural (unstraightened). This gives the renter a chance to exclaim, "It's so different!" which is always a great conversation starter. If you have straightened hair, you might try giving it some decorative flair—braids, beads, or a wrap. Renters are quite drawn to shiny colorful objects.

STICKY FINGERS

People will be touching your hair. Style it in a way that will delight curious fingers. And remember, don't overmoisturize that day!

Can I Get a Witness?

Often renters want a rental to testify to the black experience in front of an attentive crowd. This moment can be a great source of entertainment to your renter, but it can be fun for you as well. A few choice let-me-tell-you-how-it-really-is moments can make a big impact on a gathering. Choose wisely: they will be repeating to their friends everything they learned from that interesting black person at the party. "She said black people really do get tan," or "The black person I met said he's never used drugs. And I think he was telling the truth."

Feel free to embellish your own tales or create elaborate new ones for these moments when you have everyone's ear. Spin stories about leaving the ghetto, working five jobs to pay for school, and pulling yourself up by your merits and hard work. Describe in vivid detail how you grew up poor and now you drive through the old neighborhood in your SUV. Sometimes you even lock your doors. Tell the story of how your father abandoned your family when you were just a kid. Pull out the photo of your child when you affirm your promise that you will be a dedicated parent.

Tell a fun anecdote passed down through the generations of your family. Make sure it includes something about how your ancestors were freed from slavery through the Underground Railroad and would never have survived if it weren't for sympathetic white people. Reveal that you are the first person in your family to go to college, finish high school, leave the neighborhood, travel abroad, or do almost anything else. These tales can be true, based on truth, or complete fiction. It really doesn't matter to renters, who usually want colorful validation of their already extant perceptions about black people, not actual facts. Anyway, you can't change age-old ideas in one evening, and that's not in your contract.

Try not to act contrary to popular notions about black people. If you don't fit your renter's preconceptions, the renter may become confused and might dismiss you as angry. A creative renter may simply write your story for you. "Isn't it true that you almost drowned because black people can't swim, and a white lifeguard saved you and you've felt indebted to white people ever since?" Don't get backed into a corner like that. If you come with your story prepared, at least you'll be in control of the details.

If you are in a playful mood and want to shake things up a bit, there is one way playing the race card can be lots of fun. Keep a few stories of discrimination handy. Tell the story of how you were refused service at a restaurant because of your race. Your renters can express chic disgust at the treatment your people have received. They will love having the chance to distance themselves from such barbaric behavior. Obviously, they could never be racist, you're standing right there! This fail-safe rebuke of racism is often followed by asking you if you want more dessert or another cup of coffee. Say yes. Serving you that extra cup of coffee does a lot to soothe white guilt.

TELLING TALES

Truth is relative.

If you learned one thing in American history class, it was that truth is in the hands of the teller.

Don't worry about telling the truth. Give your renter what they expect from a black person. That's what they paid for.

Curb Your Knowledge

Revealing your intellect can lead to embarrassment for the client, no matter how positive your smarts might seem to you. Many rentals learn this as children. You may be familiar (even experienced) with the classic rental request that a black child produce lower grades and test scores than his or her white counterparts. As a general rule, renters expect you to answer questions about being black and ask questions about everything else.

TASTEFUL TIP

Avoid asking your renter about the secrets to their financial success, about purchasing the home next door to them, or about dating their children. There are some things renters just don't want to share.

Knowing this, a well-placed question can put your renter at ease and result in repeat rentals for you. Ask your renter benign questions about polite subjects—"Can you tell me about your garden? I want to make some time to garden when I'm not volunteering at the youth center." Or—"Is that a photo of the Great Wall? I've always wanted to go to China." (Don't let on that you've been to China twice or that you're fluent in Mandarin and Cantonese.) Allow yourself to bask in the attention generated by your inquiry. Not one for questions? Try the simple tactic of looking admiringly at the renter's collection of mallard ducks or commemorative presidential inauguration plates. It won't take long for your renter to notice your charming curiosity and start up a lively renter-centered conversation.

Some adventurous renters want to verbally spar with their rental. This is an exciting and exhausting rental to fulfill. If you are there to stimulate and challenge, make sure you have hammered out those details in your rental contract. Renters usually have specific ideas about what they expect and want to hear in a debate. Curbing your knowledge may come in handy. You don't want to find yourself accused of making things too intellectual. If the renter is dissatisfied, he might choose to replace you with someone who fits his notions of what a rental should be. If you want to cultivate a long-term rental relationship, leave the Phi Beta Kappa at home.

The Customer Is Always Right

This is a basic rule of any thriving business. Even when the customer is incorrect, it benefits a business to validate your customer's perspective. Many profitable companies have boomed due to strict adherence to this rule. As an independent contractor, you should take this premise very seriously. "Black people are so angry" is one of the most common reasons people give for putting off integrating their lives. Potential renters can project anger onto almost any comment, look, or twitch in a rental's eye. Be careful to make your renter feel secure that you aren't going to cause any disruption.

Even the smallest disagreements have been at the root of this antagonistic perception. Most of these arguments begin with seemingly harmless banter about the historical record or cultural icons. (See "Talking the Talk" for a detailed list of subjects to avoid.) Due to incongruent interpretation of facts, these topics often lead to lengthy disputes that rarely come to any resolution. This can be a bit of a downer for your host. Renters leave these experiences feeling judged, frustrated, and unsure if black people really can fit into their lives. They ask themselves, "Is it worth all the grief and hassle?"

Remember, renters are used to being credited for most of the world's significant achievements. You'd hate to undermine that kind of security. Try to gauge your renter's tolerance for reality and keep your corrections to a minimum. A handy rule is to agree with a renter nine times out of ten. If you accidentally outsmart them, you might not get their repeat business.

BITE YOUR TONGUE

You want your renters feeling good about themselves after your interactions with them. This is the best way to help them feel good about you. You're not there to further political issues or start the second wave of the civil rights movement. Forget about the debate team awards and learn how to smile and nod.

Talking the Talk: The Subjects of Conversation

After a few experiences, you will learn to cheerfully avoid certain topics while on a rental. It's not that you don't feel passionately about these subjects, it's just that discussing them rarely leads to both renter and rental feeling good about the interaction. Renters often have elaborate and eccentric ideas about these subjects or haven't thought about them at all. This can lead to either heated, lengthy conversations or an awkwardly silent room. In general it's advisable to let the client drive the conversation while you follow along. But this can lead down some squirrelly paths. As a road map, here are some subjects to keep off the table. Should they come up, it might be a nice time to excuse yourself to the restroom or answer an unexpected call on your cellular phone.

- Reparations for slavery
- The insufficient number of black people in college
- White affirmative action: legacies, donations, networking, and the general belief that white people are smarter than black people

- Gentrification
- The disproportionate number of black people in poverty
- Slavery in the "negative" sense: try to avoid words such as genocide, capture, torture, brutality, barbarism, two centuries (see the next section, "Know When to Evoke Slavery")
- Mickey Mouse
- The disproportionate number of black people in prison
- The role of racism in convicting innocent black people
- The fact that most criminals in this country are white
- Elvis Presley
- The disproportionate number of black people in the service industry
- How the unpaid labor of black people is the foundation for the economic success of the United States
- The police (though the band The Police might be a fine topic. Renters love Sting.)
- Suffocating stereotypes
- The insufficient number of black homeowners
- Black comedians
- Al Jolson (you'd be surprised how often he comes up)
- The racist thing your renter just said
- The Emancipation Proclamation
- The disproportionate number of black people in demeaning roles in the media
- The Beatles
- The insufficient number of black business owners
- The drug problem plaguing upper-middle-class white neighborhoods
- The government's racist policies
- Racial profiling
- The Alamo

Add your own topics.

Other:

_____

Other:

_____

Other:

_____

Other:

_____

NOTABLE EXCEPTION

Once in a while you may encounter renters who are genuinely interested in openly discussing these topics. They may even attentively listen as a black person shares his or her experiences. Kudos to these rare and special renters.

However, as a general rule, try to limit high-information-volume rentals to one-on-one encounters. Put a time limit on the interrogation. You don't want to be questioned for longer than an hour or two. Finally, try to schedule the rental over lunch in a public place. This will keep the tone civilized and fill your belly at the same time.

It is a good idea
to reserve the
right to bring a
white escort to
any event.

Know When to Evoke Slavery

Yes, the history of enslaved Africans in the United States is a dicey conversation topic. In fact, it's on the list of topics you might want to avoid. However, there is a place and time for everything, and oppressive historical legacies are no exception. Your ancestors didn't endure all that suffering so you'd forget about it. Use it to your advantage. There are ways you can evoke slavery, with savvy, to the satisfaction of all.

Rather than harp on the fact that African Americans suffered over two hundred years of forced labor, brutality, and near-death conditions, consider juxtaposing that difficulty with the clear and calm presence of your success. The minds of renters can be put at ease if you remind them that even though your ancestors were stolen from their land, chained, tortured, raped, beaten, and forced to work under the harshest of conditions, you now only work nine to five, rent your own home, and take two weeks of vacation a year. Things sure have changed, and it's a relief to everyone.

So, instead of discussing the current legacy of inequality left by slavery, relegate the past to the past and draw attention to your accomplishments. It can be handy to say things like, "When I signed the deed to my house, I remembered how my grandfather signed his name with an X." Perhaps chime in with "My great-grandfather was a sharecropper, and it's so great that now I can choose to eat or sell the vegetables from my own garden." Or the classic, "Standing here with you, I almost forget that my ancestors came here on the Middle Passage."

These small historical tidbits, while crediting your hardworking stock, assure renters that your presence in their lives, like your ancestors' freedom, is a gift from them. This may generate boastful responses like, "My ancestors spoke out against slavery," or "I've always been a supporter of civil rights." Renters want to connect with your achievements, even take credit for them. Don't let your pride get in the way of your paycheck. Allowing them this small liberty can lead to future rentals for you.

Study Up on Pop Culture

It is probably impossible to count the number of times you've heard a renter say, "I just saw this movie that I know you're going to love. It deals with a lot of important issues and I just know you'd like it." Usually they repeat this several times. This is "renter code" for "I just saw a movie with a black character and I've been waiting a whole week to tell someone black about it." Renters often investigate black people in a safe arena like movies or books before their first in-person interaction. As a result they often begin conversations by asking you if you've seen the movie they just saw. They figure you've seen all the movies with black people in them. They are usually referring to the latest Hollywood blockbuster with a black actor, usually someone well known, or the movie based on a historical event or a book by a popular black writer. The director of these movies is usually white.

You'll know which movies will come up in conversation, since there's usually only one or two a year to choose from. Plus, renters can usually only name three or four black actors, so it won't be hard to predict which movies they're going to ask you about. They won't ask you about foreign films, art-house films, or documentaries. They won't ask you about the latest advances in animation, your opinion of the skills of the actors, or any of the books that films are based on. They'll assume you have no interest in those things, so don't waste time overpreparing. Just take a quick trip to the video store and read the back of almost any movie box that has a black actor on the cover (often this actor is standing behind the white star or the photo is on the back of the box). That will probably be enough. You can use your imagination to fill in the predictable plot and expected role the black actor played. If you don't have time to peruse the local video store, use the flowchart on the next page.

You may not think the movie in question is an accurate representation of black people or even a decent adventure in cinematic artistry, but keep your opinions under wraps. Remember, always agree with your renters. They want to bond with you. Follow their lead. This is not the place to bring up the racial stereotypes that suffocate black actors. This is not the time to point out that vaudevillian images remain the cornerstone of black characterizations. Nor is this an opportunity to question the economic hindrances facing black filmmakers. Just smile and tell them you enjoyed the movie.

Note: If the movie is a comedy, the black person usually spends the entire time making a mockery of themselves through racial buffoonery, often involving physical stunts and distorted dialect. Historically, this has been called *minstrelsy.* These days people resist such judgmental terms and prefer to just call the actions *funny.* Renters will often say, "The movie made fun of everybody regardless of race," as they describe the slapstick display and repeat (and repeat) the mockery of language used in the film.

COMMON PLOT FOR MOVIES WITH BLACK CHARACTERS

A poor/unrefined/urban/criminal/ addicted black person often referred to by a singular first name or nickname . . .

⇒ . . . meets/is befriended by/assigned to a white person who has never spent more than an hour with a black person.

⇓

Like a beam of sunlight through the clouds, ideas about racial harmony and understanding begin to pierce through the prejudices they've each secretly harbored all their lives.

⇐ The two are challenged by a drama or adventure that forges a bond between them reminiscent of the interracial pop anthem "Ebony and Ivory."

⇓

Somewhere, deep in the crevices of their hearts, a strange churning occurs. They think they might care about each other.

⇒ As the audience develops compassion for the once downtrodden black character, the person is physically injured while experiencing a humiliating moment of racism, reducing the black character to the status of a lame workhorse.

⇓

Despite his or her best efforts, the black person dies/is killed/ is arrested/recognizes he doesn't fit in the white person's world. Note: the black person may die at any point in the movie. After a quick and tidy grieving process (which can be missed if you exit to use the restroom), the white person pulls his or herself together and becomes the star and hero of the film.

⇐ Despite her or his best efforts, the white person is unable to help the new black friend survive the crippling injury and racist humiliation.

A small yet nagging hope remains that their lives were altered by this brief, yet meaningful interlude. The characters and the audience wonder if they will be nicer to people of other races in the future. Just as this thought is suggested, the film shows that this requires effort and commitment, and so is an impractical idea.

⇓

OR.
The two part ways realizing the age-old truth that their relationship could only be a result of extraordinary circumstances. They wake up, much like Dorothy in *The Wizard of Oz*, to realize that their brilliant Technicolor world has returned to black and white.

⇒

⇓

The two part ways knowing they will never speak of their encounter to anyone in their lives. The people back home don't understand or believe their story. Once in a while, when they see a person of another race walking on the other side of the street, they smile to themselves.

END

If you don't have time to study up on the latest re-staging of this classic plot, don't worry. You can wing it through a conversation with a few well-placed questions and a convincing look of sincere intrigue. You can always ask the renter to tell you all the details of the movie and their insights. They will be more than happy to oblige. They may even feel pretty advanced to have seen it before you. They might suggest that they take you to see it. That means another rental for you.

Hobbies Anyone?

What did you do with your day off?

Think this is an easy question to answer? Guess again.

Don't say: I spent the morning brushing up on my French in preparation for my annual trip to Europe this fall. Then I updated my portfolio with a few hot stocks I've been watching. Then for dinner I tried out a new veal recipe, given to me by my neighbor who is the executive chef of a world-famous Italian restaurant.

Do say: I spent the morning collecting donations for a church fundraiser. We're hoping to raise enough to send one of us to bring our church teachings to Africa. I sure hope I get to go to Africa one day, since it is my homeland. I called my mother like I do every week. I had a craving for her famous pork-fried collard greens, so I asked her for the recipe. Then I read a magazine and paid half of a stack of bills.

Don't say: I spent the weekend studying my favorite classical symphonies and searching for a rare collection of the poems of Lao Tzu. Then I went to volunteer at the school for the deaf, which was lovely because I so enjoy using sign language. And I finally got a chance to take in the jazz club that just opened down the street from you. The food and the music were both exquisite.

Do say: I spent the weekend playing b-ball at the public park in my old neighborhood, and chillin' with my peeps. After that I caught up on some work that my boss wants finished by Monday and called

Don't say: I was studying my favorite artist.

Do say: I was reading old slave narratives.

my mother like I do every week. I made sure my kids did their homework, watched television, and got ready for another work week.

Don't say: I worked most of the day on a short story. It will be my third published in an international journal. I talked to a friend of mine in Amsterdam, then finished the evening by curling up with some Miles Davis, a Sam Shepard play, and a crème brûlée in front of the fire.

Do say: Several of us from the old neighborhood got together to paint over graffiti and clean up the streets. Then I met up with the youth I sponsor from the Big Brothers/Big Sisters program. I called my mother like I do every week. At night I rewatched a history of black America movie. It's my favorite. I've seen it six times now.

Don't say: I decided to take a day and do all the things my dad taught me when I was a child. First I cooked a big breakfast for my whole family. Then I made several copper etchings and did some research on a scientific principle I've been curious about. By the end of the day I was ready to relax with my father's favorite book of philosophy. It was just like being home again.

Do say: Man, I didn't do anything at all. I sat around all day just doing nothing. It was great. Just like my old man . . . when he was around. I forgot to call my mother, so she got mad and called me. After she finished yelling, I sweet-talked her into baking me one of her famous pies.

Don't say: I went for a nature walk with my organic gardening group and stopped in for a latte at the café my friend owns. When I got home, I fixed a vegan meal for me and my best friend, and we spent the evening discussing plans for our environmental action group.

Do say: I spent the morning washing and waxing my car. I went to my neighborhood bar where I watched the game and drank all afternoon with my friends. I called my mother like I do every week and my "baby" cooked up a big roast beef dinner. It was so good I ate too much and fell asleep on the couch.

Being a rent-a-negro means you're in the business of supply and demand. Give the people want they want or your market might dry

Don't.

Do.

up. You may have innovative ideas about what will truly benefit your customers, but new and fresh ideas have to be introduced slowly, over time. You don't want your renters to be put off by your unconventional product. They might turn to your competition. Once you have loyal customers, you can experiment. Then, if you want to market a new updated form of rent-a-negro, you can launch a test product to a limited group rather than changing your entire service line.

MOM'S FAVORITE TIP

Renters love to hear about your mother. They often say, "I'd love to meet your mother. She must be a fascinating woman!" Always try to work a story about your mom into your rental conversations.

Role Models

Have you noticed a peculiar fascination among your renters with black role models? You aren't alone. Though the roots of this enthrallment have yet to be determined, there is a method for addressing this issue while avoiding confusion and controversy. When a renter asks, "So, when you were growing up, who were your role models?" you might feel perplexed. Is the renter asking about the people who helped you combat the perils of racism and oppression— that ugly conversational topic you've spent the whole night minimizing? Clearly, this can become a tricky question to navigate.

Keep in mind that the renter may already assume that you had very few positive immediate influences on your life. If you talk about your father or your college professor, you might lose the renter's attention. If the renter thinks you had an easy life, he or she may start to question your blackness. Many rentals over the years have creatively embellished details about their background for just this reason. As a safe bet, you can always say, "My main role model is my mother [or grandmother] who worked so hard to raise so many [eight or more] children all by herself, with no education or help." This answer always seems to get a winning response from renters. They often chime in with, "I thought you might say that. I'm sure she's a very strong woman. She must have worked like an ox."

When searching for other names to list, choose people who are obvious. Your renter will want to recognize the personality. If you pick someone without instant name recognition, it might stun your renter and you might come across as just a bit smarter than what they paid for.

HEROIC TIP

When asked to list your role models, choose nonviolent, nonmilitant political leaders: Martin Luther King Jr., not Malcolm X. It's best to look proud of your race without appearing intimidating.

Is your renter starting to look confused, dazed? Is their attention starting to drift? Think back, did you make the mistake of naming people outside of your race? No, no, don't do that. Quick, go back. Name only black people. That should take that puzzled look off their face. It's confusing to renters to think that you might admire a white, Asian, or Latino person or anyone who doesn't look like you. You don't want them to think that you've widened your horizons before you met them. They might want to help you reach beyond what you know, expose you to a broader culture, which means more rentals for you. So don't mention that Russian writer, Japanese actor, or Mexican revolutionary, no matter how much you have modeled your life after his work. Keep it simple. Stick to your own kind.

Renters often go out of their way to make watermelon available at events when they know you are coming. You will have to make your own decision about this socially loaded food.

Watermelon and Fried Chicken: To Eat or Not to Eat, That Is the Question

Believe it or not, the popular perception that black people have a passion for watermelon and fried chicken is tenaciously intact. Do you feel pressure to jump to your feet and squeal with delight when you are offered either of these foods by a renter? When you don't jump and squeal, you may find yourself staring back at a room full of disappointed faces. The sloppy-food-lovin' legacy lingers from the days of stage and film minstrelsy. Antics ensued as a result of the insatiable appetites of black characters. They chased after greasy, drippy food with the same fervor and futility they chased white people as sexual objects. The laughter never stopped. Today, even the most sophisticated renters try to re-create these much-loved images.

Renters often go out of their way to make watermelon available at events when they know you are coming. They are extraordinarily enthusiastic about presenting it at parties and gatherings. Renters themselves seem to be avid consumers of watermelon and constantly rave about the taste. There is no conclusive evidence that renters eat watermelon quite as much or as often when they are by themselves or that this behavior is just a ploy to increase the chances that you might partake of their offerings. Renters' pro-watermelon behavior may be heightened as a result of any black presence and renters' desire to cater to your tastes and interests. So, be aware that should you turn down the salacious, seedy fruit, you may be met with shock or disbelief and even find that you've insulted the efforts of your host. You are likely to hear the phrase, "What? *You* don't like watermelon?!"

This can be an awkward situation. As a quick remedy here are some simple methods for diffusing the hysteria:

1. Claim to have a rare genetic allergy to the precious fruit.

2. Opt for a different melon on the menu (cantaloupe is always nice).

3. If the situation becomes desperate, you can, with practice, develop a tolerance for the fruit and the satisfied smiles and knowing nudges that accompany your public consumption of it.

Similar approaches can be applied to the public eating of fried chicken, another favorite served by renters attempting to accommodate your ethnic palette. Some rentals have instituted a strict policy against the consumption of watermelon and fried chicken. You will have to make your own decisions about these socially loaded foods, but be advised, one bite may be followed by a request to paint your face black and break into a song and dance about your mammy.

A Sexy Side Note

Is it true? Do black girls just want to get f**ked all night? Are black men really "bigger, bolder, better?" However distasteful, legends of black sexuality persist and the topic does find its way into conversation.

It is not uncommon to field these questions from renters. You may even receive requests to fulfill a range of athletic sexual services rumored to be practiced by black people. In fact, these requests are frequently made, particularly at a party after your renter has had a few drinks. For your own safety, you might want to limit your alcohol intake so you can remain professional, make rational decisions, and easily find your way to the nearest exit. But don't get too worried. For the most part, as renters will tell you, these questions simply demonstrate a genuine curiosity about black people. Your renter may have heard a story or two and has the rare opportunity to discover if the rumors hold any truth.

The sexuality of black people is an ancient mystery that plagues the minds of renters worldwide. As such, questions abound and can spill out in the middle of civilized conversation. It's difficult for some renters to control their appetites for information. Like children, their curiosity can get the better of them and before you know it, they're sneaking sideways glances at your pants zipper or the middle button on your blouse. Learn to forgive and forget. They aren't always aware that asking someone they've just met about the size of their sexual appetite or sexual organs might be slightly indiscreet. They don't intend to do you or your virtue any harm.

Should a proposition be made, simply explain to your renter that, in most states, exchanging sexual services for money is illegal. Remind the renter that this is not listed on your invoice. There are plenty of agencies that specialize in those services and are happy to fulfill whatever perverse pleasure your renter harbors. Should the renter still insist on hearing answers to provocative questions, you can avoid an awkward conflict by simply saying that some things should remain a mystery and excusing yourself to make a phone call.

Check Your Sense of Outrage at the Door

It's important to project a sense of calm and composure as a rental. This way you maintain your inner peace and allow your client to be at ease throughout the event. Comfort is one of the basic services you are providing as a rent-a-negro. Remember, good intentions are one of your renters' greatest motivating factors. It's very common for renters to say, "But I wasn't trying to offend anyone. I just don't know any better. I'm genuinely trying to learn."

Are you going to be offended at some point during the event? Probably. But that's no different than any other day, so why let it get to you? Plus, don't forget, you're on the clock. If you were doing this work for free, you'd have every right to challenge, expose, and contradict at every turn. But that confrontation can't buy you a new pair of shoes. That argument might drain the energy you need to finish building that addition on your house. Don't let your anger get in the way of a solid paycheck. If your sense of outrage can't be tempered, perhaps you ought to find a different line of work.

Here's something that can help. When you go to an event, take a moment to pause before you enter. Take deep breaths. Visualize

SURVIVAL TIP

Just in case you can't let go of your sense of outrage so easily, try playing a little game with yourself. Keep track of offensive and ignorant comments. Did this event have more or less comments than the last one? Was there one particularly creative insult that you've never heard before? You and other rentals can start an Offensive Remark Hall of Fame. You can give points for originality. Maybe even start a pool to see who hears the most or the strangest quips. You might make a little extra money with a good side bet.

checking your sense of outrage at the door, like an overcoat. It'll be there when you get back. Just because you didn't have it for a few hours doesn't mean it was lost. In fact, it might feel pretty good to slip on that overcoat of outrage as you leave a long night of being rented.

Remember, renters worry that black people are ready to fly off the handle at the slightest offense. That's one of the reasons they invited you to their party instead of taking a risk with an unpaid black person. You are a professional. You are there to enhance the atmosphere. This takes a delicate touch. Your renter wants to feel safe, comfortable, and able to speak freely. One of the most common comments from satisfied renters is, "I felt so *comfortable*. I never thought it could be so easy being around a black person." Offering the renter this kind of experience will generate positive feedback and lead to more rental work for you.

Honey, I Have a Headache

Tired? Feeling emotionally neglected? Just not in the mood? Sometimes you need some attention and care before you can fulfill requests for professional black services. You can't always jump into a rental with someone you just met. Some days you just wish people wanted to know about the real you, that they didn't want you just for your rental skills. It is at these moments when a determined quickie renter can just about send you over the edge.

You've tried to politely decline. "Actually, I don't feel like answering that question right now." Often these wishes are ignored or, worse, are met with indignation: "What's the big deal? I just asked a simple question. You shouldn't be so rude."

To avoid this uncomfortable and often futile exchange, try a fresh and fun approach. It's recommended that you do not use these techniques with regularity or you might damage your reputation as a reliable rental. But once in a while, it's OK to have some fun. Here are some easy ways to diffuse the fervor of a demanding renter.

Use these in those moments when you just can't do one more on-the-spot rental.

The example below uses the common insta-rental question: "How do you wash your hair?"

1. Play dumb.

   "I don't know. Gee, what do you think I should do? How do you wash *your* hair?"

2. Give useless information.

   "First I finagle the hypodermology, then use a directionality of the perimorphism, and lastly optimize the zenadirith. Usually that's all it takes."

3. Involve the renter in the question to a degree that will make the person uncomfortable.

   "I'm so glad you asked me. I haven't washed my hair in months. I could really use some help. It's not that dirty and it'll only take about five hours. Are you available?"

4. Turn the tables.

   "I'm always so surprised at how many white people ask me this. I thought you were a much more hygienic people, but I'm learning that soap and water is a new concept for you folks."

You don't want to use these approaches with your regular paying clientele. These are to be reserved for pesky on-demand rentals who are as persistent as you are drained. It's OK to take a rental break every once in a while. The market won't dry up if you refuse an occasional request. You can be assured that tomorrow, someone new will come along with the same question.

Tools of the Trade: Rental Resources

Now that you've discovered that you are a rental, you may be calculating the amount of money you've missed from all the work you've done without payment. Never fear! The remedy is easy: start getting paid! You can make honest consumers out of your community members by using these few simple tools.

Playing by the Rules: Guidelines for Your Renters

A sound contract ensures a successful rental. Make sure your bases are covered by asking your renter to agree to these simple terms. A willingness to sign the contract will demonstrate trust and good business ethics while ensuring a healthy exchange between you and your renter. Here are some suggestions to include in your contract:

- 50 percent of payment is required as a deposit.
- Remainder of payment is due at the time of the renting.
- One pre-rent evaluation may be requested by the rental.
- Services rendered not listed in contract will be charged at the end of an event (keep a running tab of every service you provide).
- The rental reserves the right to bring a white escort to any event.
- Exits must be clearly marked and remain unobstructed.
- Rental's dietary requirements must be met.
- Rental will take a private ten-minute break every hour.
- Rental must be returned intact, in his or her original condition.

- Travel expenses over fifty miles to and from the event will be paid for in advance by renter.
- Accommodations for events that require an overnight stay will be paid for in advance by renter, including hotel and meal costs. Accommodations must be private and in a separate location from the rental event.
- Payment is nonrefundable. Terminated contracts will not be refunded.
- The rental reserves the right to refuse service to anyone.

Card Carrying: Authentic African American Business Card

Once in a while a renter might ask "Are you saying that because you're black or are you just saying that?" It's an awkward question that can be settled with the presentation of a small bit of paperwork. The renter is asking you if your life experiences qualify you to make statements as a black person, or if you are some kind of exception or imposter. Don't let this faze you. If a person offered his opinion on your sore back, you'd make sure he was a certified professional, wouldn't you? Calmly reassure your skeptical renter that you indeed are an authentic black person and that you have the credentials to prove it.

For these moments you might consider carrying a simple business card that certifies your blackness and can assure anyone you meet of your authenticity. This way you can confidently guarantee people that you are qualified to comment on any and all aspects of your life as a black person. Should they express further concern about your authenticity, you may need to go the extra step of carrying a copy of your birth certificate. Once they see this they can be certain that you were officially certified as African American at birth.

Your Name _____

Authentic African American

Over _____ Years of Experience

Certified at Birth,
City, State USA _____

Copy this image and have your own cards printed with your name, years of experience, and birthplace. If you like, you can include your rental contact information right on your card. You might want to make several hundred business cards. Once you start handing them out, they go quickly.

Carry your card at all times. Keep it in your wallet or purse for easy access. This way, should anyone question your expertise, you can easily pull out the "race card" and reassure doubters that you are a trained and experienced professional.

Copy the invoice below to give to your prospective renters.

rent-a-negro

INVOICE

Billed to: _____

Address: _____

Phone: _____

Email: _____

Date of Rental: _____ Date of Invoice: _____

☐ Corporate/business rate = $350/hour x _____ hours = $_____

☐ Personal/private/individual rate = $200/hour x _____ hours = $_____

☐ Drop-in/appearances $100 each x _____ appearances = $_____

☐ Informational/high question volume = additional $100/hour x _____ hours = $_____

☐ Ongoing/retainer services = $10,000 annually

ADDITIONAL SERVICES

☐ Provide a black opinion = $75 per call/email x _____ times = $_____

☐ Let you touch my hair = $100 per touch x _____ times = $_____

☐ Let you touch my skin = $75 per touch x _____ times = $_____

☐ Compare skin tones = $100 per comparison x _____ times = $_____

☐ Let you tell me, "You look just like . . ." = $100 x _____ times = $_____

☐ Let you call me "sista/brotha" or "girlfriend/homey" or "girl/man" = $150 x _____ times = $_____

☐ Play the name game = $35 per rhyme x _____ rhymes = $_____

☐ Give dance lessons to the rhythmically challenged = $250/hour x _____ hours

☐ Challenge racist family members = additional $500 per event

☐ Provide a "Tell them I'm not a racist" vouch = $1500 per vouch x _____ times = $_____

☐ Be silent and "Just let it go" = $1,000 each time x _____ times = $_____

☐ Other service: _____ = $_____

☐ Other service: _____ = $_____

☐ Other service: _____ = $_____

TOTAL THIS INVOICE: $_____

Signed (Renter): _____

Signed: (Rental): _____

Is this part of a retroactive billing program? ☐ Yes ☐ No

Does 5% discount apply? ☐ Yes ☐ No

White Noise: Common Questions You'll Have to Answer

"White noise" is the term for sounds that are such a regular part of your environment that they blend into a dependable background hum. White noise is a subtle sound track for your daily life. It's like living next to a freeway. At first, the sound of the cars may seem so loud you can barely hear yourself think. But after a while the drone becomes familiar, a standard part of your daily routine. In fact, some days you can't imagine living without it. Just kidding.

These questions and comments are some of the most frequent and choice chatter collected from renters. The banter below is just some of the talk that makes up the white noise of many renters' daily existence. The comments are collected below so you can refresh your reactions. You may have heard these statements so often that you've begun to tune them out. It's time to splash some cold water on your face and listen again to what's being said around you. You don't want a stale expression coming over your face in the middle of a rental. You don't want your renters to think they're boring you. In fact, many renters may think that this is the first time you've heard anyone say these things. So, stay alert and stay interested.

- "Do black people get tan? What I mean is, does your skin get darker? And then do you call that 'tan' or 'darker'? You get blacker, right? Or do you get lighter? Do you get lighter in the sun?"

- "You speak English very well. You're so articulate. You can talk without even sounding black. But you could sound black if you wanted to, right? Do it now. Say something and sound really black."

- "I used to try to make friends with black people, but black people just don't want to be friends with white people. I try to talk to them and they look at me like I'm crazy. What am I doing wrong?"
- "I thought it would be really fascinating to meet you since you're from the Caribbean. Oh, you're not from the Caribbean? Well, you could be. Are you sure you're not?"
- "I've met a few black people in my life. They were interesting, always wore the most colorful clothes. I don't remember their names. I liked to look at them. But I didn't make friends with any of them. We didn't have anything in common."
- "How come black people don't come to our group? I invite them. I have food I think they will like, but they don't come. Week after week we wait, and no people of color come. They just aren't interested in our group. I guess we're going to stay an all-white group. I don't know how to change that. It's not our fault. We want to talk about racism, but how can we do that without people of color there?"
- "Why do you call yourselves black? I mean you're not really black, you're more of a brown color. Though I did see this man once who was so black. He was actually black, like the color, like my shoes. Actually black. He was beautiful. I thought so."
- "You have such an interesting name. Are you named after [insert name of geographical landmark] or [insert name of ethnic food] or maybe [insert rhyming name of impoverished country]? I've never met anyone with your name. Did you make it up yourself?"
- "Why are you always talking about racism? Can't you just relax? I tell people not to talk about race around black people 'cause you'll get really angry and call them racist."
- "I really don't have very much experience with people of color. I don't know what to say or do. I'm from an all-white town, remember? Don't fault me for my circumstances. If I'm

Have a friend or fellow rental read these questions aloud. Practice expressing surprise and pleasure at the earnest curiosity of the asker. Pretend you are hearing these comments for the first time. (It may take several tries.)

surrounded by white people, I'm going to know mostly white people and know about white people. What am I supposed to do? Yes, all of my friends are white, but I don't know any other people. Am I supposed to seek out black people? You think they're going to talk to me?"

- "My grandparents are the most racist people you'd ever meet. I sit at dinner sometimes and they say the most racist things. I can't believe it. There's nothing I can do about it. Let me tell you some of the things they say. They are so racist."

- "Last year I read this book, I don't remember the name, but a black person wrote it. You know the one they made into a movie? It was great. You'd like it. It wasn't like anything I've ever read. You'd probably understand it more than I would. It was really good. The main character was black and he killed a woman and he was running from the police. And I don't want to spoil the ending or anything 'cause you really should read it, but he gets killed. In the end. In prison. He was guilty. It was really good. Really realistic. A black person wrote it, so it was accurate. I think it was based on a true story. I bet it was true. You'd like it. You should read it. I'll lend it to you."

- "Where I went to school there was a lot of racism and the black kids were always protesting. I don't really know much about it. I heard once that the campus police beat this kid up because he was black. But he must have done something wrong. Anyway, I didn't really get involved with it. I had to concentrate on important things, like my schoolwork."

- "All the black people I've met are so angry, it makes it hard to be friends with them. But you are easy to talk to. You don't get mad every time I say something."

- "You come from a big family. And you grew up in the ghetto, I mean, inner city. Right? How many brothers and sisters do you have? Did you have to share a bedroom with all of them? Do you know your father? And you were really poor and on welfare. Or did you have money? Then you aren't *really* black. Like, you are black, but you are kind of white too. You kind of act white. I bet you can be black or white depending on who you are talking to."

- "Were your great-grandparents slaves? I just found out that my great-great-grandparents were slave masters. They owned slaves. Of course I don't think that's good or anything. I'm glad that it's all in the past now. I can't be held responsible for something my ancestors did hundreds of years ago. It was a really long time ago.

Everything is different now. People are equal. I can't keep paying for things my ancestors did that I don't even believe in. What am I supposed to do, pay a special tax? A white tax?"

- "People think that you, I mean black people, are uneducated. But you're different. I mean, I don't think of you that way. A lot of people I know think that way. You're easy to talk to. Most black people aren't as easy to talk to as you are. I can say whatever I want around you and I know you're not going to call me a racist or something. Right? Because I'm not. I'm not a racist. You know that, right?"

- "I don't even see race. When I look at someone I don't see their race at all. I'm really beyond all of that."

- "I don't think of you as black."

Sailing Through the Stress:
Wellness Techniques

Stress is one of the main side-effects of operating any successful business. If you hope to succeed at your work while retaining enough energy to enjoy the rest of your life, you have to learn how to de-stress. Take some time now to incorporate a regular routine of self-care into your weekly schedule. Even rental events can provide opportunities to care for yourself. Take ten minutes to meditate before you start a rental. If you are dealing with an impulse renter, count to ten before you engage. Wash your hands regularly, eat healthful foods, and treat yourself to a healing indulgence every once in a while. After all, your body and mind are the instruments of your success. Taking care of yourself is a critical part of remaining a vibrant rental who is able to contribute to your community with joy and vitality.

Dealing with life as a black person is a unique challenge already, as the study below demonstrates.

Invented circa 2000 by A. J. Patterson, The Collar was designed to familiarize white people, in some small way, with the daily experiences of racism common for people of color in our society.

Designed to attach to any number of everyday fashions, The Collar was lined with a low-voltage electrical shock wire, similar to those used on farms to keep animals from going astray. The wire, cleverly concealed by the fabric of the collar, emits a short, yet biting burst of electrical voltage whenever the wearer encounters an example of racism. Though physical shock cannot accurately mimic the true effect of racism on people of color, The Collar gave a parallel sensation that at the very least drew attention to the frequency of such experiences in the wearer's environment.

Initial production of The Collar was terminated during the experimental phase when a trial was done with a large white test group and a control group of people of color. Though the control group found the device to be accurate, the white group described side effects. They complained of nausea, bitterness, depression, violent and suicidal tendencies, anxiety, sleeplessness, hypertension, anger, rage, fear, withdrawal, and even periods of mild unconsciousness. After two days most white participants refused to wear the device and demanded compensation for their suffering.

Development drew to an abrupt halt.

Don't let your personal development draw to an abrupt halt. Learn to replenish yourself on a regular basis. Remember, if you're not healthy, you can't be rented. Massage, gym workouts, therapy, holistic healing, regular doctor visits, counseling, personal trainers, yoga classes, kickboxing, frequent vacations, organic food, entertainment, hydrotherapy, and acupuncture are just a few of the ways rentals have found to keep themselves on track and maintain a sense of self throughout a lifetime of rental activity. Have fun and experiment. But remember, many of these outlets come at a cost. Let's face it, most services in this world just aren't free. Make sure your rental prices account for the cost of regular stress relief.

Cash-or Check Only: Charging for Your Services

Nervous about charging your renters? You've noticed that not every-one freely admits to being a renter. Will people be surprised when you present them a bill? Let's examine this situation and lay your concerns to rest.

Selective Ignorance Syndrome (SIS)

Many renters claim to be unaware or unwilling to admit that they participate in the business of renting. When faced with their actions, renters may invoke a mantra much like pleading the Fifth Amendment—"I refuse to answer that question on the grounds that it might incriminate me." Others attempt to reframe their actions in a positive light. "I only did that because I wanted to make you feel comfortable, included, and important."

It can be hard to know how to respond in this situation. You may feel as if the person has suddenly entered an alternative reality. As a result, he or she may be very difficult to reach through rational dis-cussion. You may even feel as if you are losing touch with the here-and-now when your renter fades into this altered, sometimes blissful state. Don't second-guess yourself. You're not imagining things. You're witnessing the symptoms of a very serious condition that has plagued the minds of renters for centuries. This condition has been thoroughly researched and recently labeled Selective Ignorance Syndrome (SIS).

The historical foundations of this condition date back to the days of forced servitude. Not only did white people enslave blacks, they spent a great many resources trying to convince themselves that this was a legitimate practice. Things are much the same today. These days, renters' insistence that you teach them about race or racism may sound hauntingly like "Bring me my dinner, boy." Their admonishments that you should be glad that they take an interest in your culture may be reminiscent of "You should be happy to have me as your owner. Few other slaves have it so good." This becomes a daily frustration for many rentals, but don't start a revolt just yet. The invoice in your hand may be one step toward a cure.

Today, even those who claim, "My ancestors didn't own slaves," suffer from the symptoms of SIS. This shows that the disease is passed not only genetically, but it can also spread through social interaction and environmental factors. Schools and the media are sources of mass infection. Researchers are working on a prophylactic to prevent the spread of the condition, but find this a unique challenge. Governmental support for SIS research is at an all-time low. Images of black servitude and inferiority are propagating at such a rapid rate that it is hard for researchers to keep up with the adaptations and mutated strains. These images permeate the minds of renters on a daily basis from an ever-widening range of sources. Just turn on the television or go to a popular movie and you'll find at least one source of SIS. Mention this to the white person sitting next to you and you're likely to get a classic SIS response: "I never noticed that." Or, "Really? No, I see positive images of black people every day." Or, "Thanks for pointing that out. If I didn't know you, I would never know about these things."

The most important thing to do is to stay objective. SIS is a crippling condition that is easily spread. In fact, many of those suffering from it try to recruit others into their way of thinking. Try hard not to enable SIS thought patterns in your renters. Act strongly and compassionately. Simply remember that the person in front of you is coping with SIS, and issue them an invoice for any services they've procured from you. Shock therapy is one of the many experimental treatments now being investigated as a cure for SIS. Your handing them a bill might be just the jolt needed to send SIS into remission.

Standard practice requires a 50 percent deposit upon confirmation, with the remainder to be paid upon arrival at event.

Payment

It is easy and convenient to accept cash or checks for both current and retroactive services. Several online services make it easy to accept major credit cards. This can prove useful for both you and your renters. For drop-in appearances, payment should be made in full when the request is confirmed. Otherwise, standard practice requires a 50 percent deposit upon confirmation, with the remainder to be paid upon arrival at the event. Retainer services can be paid quarterly or monthly. Print an invoice for each rental you've contracted and upon payment remit a copy of that invoice stamped "paid in full." With all there is to remember as a rental, keep your billing and paper-work simple.

After Words

There Are Rentals I Remember: Stories from the Field

Below are real-life accounts of one rental's experiences from her perspective as well as the perspectives of some of her most memorable renters. Presented here in chronological order, from childhood through adulthood, each reflection offers a handy moral to aid you in your pursuit at any stage of the rental business. Whether you are a renter or a rental, these stories can help you get a feel for what renting is like from both sides of the transaction.

Names and locations have been changed to maintain confidentiality.

RENTER: Steve Harris, school principal
EVENT TYPE: Ongoing/retainer services
LOCATION: Elementary school

The rental reflects:
I am eight years old. I have been rented a lot since I was about 3. Well, maybe before then, but I can't remember anything before then. Not much anyway.

Being a rental means people ask me a lot of questions 'cause I'm the only black girl they know. I go to a lot of birthday parties. That's kind of fun. Black History Month at school is fun too. It's like I get to be the teacher for a whole month!

When I go to white kids' houses the parents always ask me if I have basic things like food or books at home. What planet do they live on? My mom has so many books I can't even count them. I bet I can't even read them all before I'm old like her. Sometimes I want to say "No, I've never owned my very own book. Can I have some of yours?" But my parents get really mad when I lie.

Anyway, so . . . oh, yeah . . . I work as a rental and also go to school and other stuff. (My parents make me take cello lessons.) For the most part I can do it all. It's a lot of work, but like I already said, I've been doing it since I can remember. It's not so bad, I guess. I'm saving up for college and a chemistry set.

OK, so like I said, its mostly fun, but sometimes I get confused. Last week my school gave my entire grade a test that they said would show how smart we are. I think they were trying to see who was smartest in the grade. They're always making us compete to see who's fastest, prettiest, and stuff.

But they forgot to tell me I was supposed to do bad on the test. So I did my best as usual. It wasn't very hard. I guess I did pretty good, because the principal said my score was too high. He said I had to take the test again.

No one told me this was a rental and that they wanted me to fail. If I was supposed to get a bad score I would have answered the questions wrong. Now everyone is mad at me because I did better than most of the white kids in the grade.

Then I find out that a white boy in my class, Todd Simon, and I have the highest scores. I guess this makes our teacher angry or something because she starts acting all strange. From that day on she keeps making Todd and me compete against each other. She says things like "I bet you can't finish this book before Todd." Or "Todd can do this math problem, why can't you?" It gets pretty annoying.

This year our whole class is learning handwriting. We all have books where we copy letters and sentences to practice our cursive. We all make it into a race to see who would finish their book first. I guess I was going to finish before Todd because as I get close to finishing my book, our teacher makes me re-do a whole page of the letter R. So of course Todd finishes before me. My teacher never even checks my page of Rs after I redo them. Then yesterday during song time the teacher points at me and says to the whole class, "Maybe she will be pretty one day when she grows up." Everyone stares at me. I feel ugly.

If someone had told me to do bad on that test, everyone would be happy and I wouldn't be getting teased by my teacher. Can everyone just calm down? I'm not trying to screw up your life here. Geez, I'm only eight. I'm just trying to get through second grade.

Next time you want me to fail a test, just tell me so. I know all the right answers, so I'll just not choose those ones. I can really blow it. I don't like failing tests, but at least my teacher will be nicer to me and I'll have lots of fun with my new chemistry set.

MORAL FOR RENTALS: Get clear instructions. Being black doesn't make you a mind reader.

RENTER: Lacy Crocker, a twelve-year-old at a summer day camp
EVENT TYPE: Individual
LOCATION: The swimming pool at a day camp
OTHER SERVICES: High question volume

The rental reflects:
This day camp didn't have very many black kids so here I am. The program is full of kids I don't know. But that's OK. Being a rental is like that. But at least at camp I get to see horses and go swimming. In wood shop I am building a coffee table that I plan to give to my parents. That's a pretty cool bonus to being a rental. Most of the money I make goes into my college fund, so this is extra. I wish I always got a piece of furniture after a gig like this. I'd have the whole house decorated by now.

On the way to camp the bus driver likes to make fun of black music on the radio. Boring. Get a new joke. Anyway, I just tune it out because there isn't much I can do about it. There's about 20 white kids on the bus who think this guy is really funny.

Camp gets a little boring too. In every class, at every meal, and in every sports game, one of the other kids makes a big deal of the fact that I am black. They like to point out how strange or different I am.

I wonder where do all these kids go to school that they never see someone black? Do they live with the horses all year round?

Anyway, it's hot and we get to go in the pool today. I'm kind of digging this camp rental thing. Pools, wood shop, games, maybe I can make it an annual job. Things are going pretty smoothly but once in a while something weird happens like today. I'm practicing underwater handstands in the pool when I come up for air and find one of the other camp girls standing right in front of me. Her name is Lacy and she's white and really, really loud. Before I say hi to her, OK, well, I don't really say hi to her, because I don't like her. Basically I just look at her, wondering why she is standing so close to me. She is with a friend. She says to her friend, "Look, her hair doesn't get wet," and she points at my head. Here we go. This is how I earn my pay.

This makes no sense to me because she saw me just come up from my cool underwater handstand. But I have to answer any and all questions about being black. So I say to her, "What do you mean? Of course it's wet. I just came up from underwater didn't you see me?" She screams, "No it's not. It's dry. Look at it!" she screams, tugging on her friend.

I'm stumped. I really don't know what to say to her. When something is put in water, it gets wet. I don't want to make her feel stupid, but what more is there to say? Maybe they didn't teach her about water in science class. Where do these kids go to school? Good grief. I learned that in kindergarten. Even though I'm sick of people grabbing my hair, I think about telling her to touch my hair so she can feel for herself that it is wet. But then it occurs to me that we are in the pool. Everything is wet including our hands. If she touched my hair she couldn't tell if it is wet or dry. My brain is turning into a pretzel trying to follow this girl. I figure that maybe if I demonstrate, she will understand the whole water = wet thing. So I dunk my head under water and when I come up I think the debate will be calmly and quietly resolved. Ta-da! See, I'm wet! Duh.

Nope. The situation is hopeless. Lacy continues to scream, "It's dry, it's dry!" I'm beginning to wonder if this has anything to do with water at all. Other kids are coming over to our spot in the pool to see what's going on. I'm starting to get nervous. I worry that the kids might try to hold me underwater to see how long it takes to get my hair wet. That's not covered in my fees. Do I have insurance for that? I know a twelve-year-old shouldn't have to think about things like insurance, but this is making me think that I need to ask my parents about that stuff. I wonder what they do in a situation like this? Just when I'm planning an escape route, a kid in a different corner pees in the pool. Everyone squeals and jumps out. Lacy runs away. I dry off and go to wood shop and make a lamp for my bedroom. Camp rentals aren't perfect, but like I said, some things are pretty cool.

MORAL FOR RENTALS: Network and make connections. For example, tip the kid who peed in the pool. You might need his help later.

RENTER: John Berger, a high school teacher of American literature
EVENT TYPE: Ongoing/retainer services
LOCATION: High school English class

The renter writes:
I am an eleventh-grade American Literature teacher. I really enjoy my work. It is so important to bring the classics of literature to the minds of young people. They really need to be exposed to the great minds of the English language. So far we've read *The Scarlet Letter, A Farewell to Arms, The Great Gatsby,* and *Billy Budd.* I am renting a couple of black students for my class because I think I can really reach out to them and broaden their minds with these classic texts.

The curriculum doesn't have any novels or short stories by black people because there weren't any that fit with the caliber of the other authors in the class. I want to make sure the black students in my class feel that their culture is valued, so we will read a few poems by black authors. I'm sure one day a black person will write something significant that I can assign to my students. Black people keep making progress. Soon a classic black novelist is sure to emerge.

This week we will read those black poems. I've chosen some that reflect the struggle and history of black people over the ages. I'm excited because I want to have the black students in the class read the poems. They will love the opportunity to represent their culture. I know they will be so proud. Plus, I haven't called on them very much this year. They just don't seem interested in the class. I'm hoping this material will feel relevant to their experience and get them engaged. I will ask them a few personal follow-up questions to show them how interested I am in them as individuals.

The first student I call on is a girl. I ask her to read the poem about slavery. After she does, I ask her what the poet means. She looks down at her book quietly. She doesn't answer. I don't understand. She must have some kind of feeling about this poem. She just read about her ancestors being beaten and tortured and worked to death. How can she just be quiet? Doesn't she think about these things? I wait as long as I can for her to respond but then I am forced to call on one of the eager white students, who has a brilliant explanation of the work. I'm disappointed in the black student. I gave her such an opportunity and she just screwed it up. Now she's staring out the window, and I'm forced to give her a bad grade. I may even have to trade her in for another rental or maybe get my money back. But that's so harsh, I'm not an insensitive person. Maybe I'll give her another chance next semester when we read *Huckleberry Finn*.

The next student I call on is a boy and has a funny name. I tell him about the tradition of naming in Africa and how it is different from the way we do things here. That's probably why his name is like that. I ask him questions and invite all the other students to ask him questions too. What a great moment. I can't wait to tell my supervisor. I've really created a great learning experience for everyone. The white students get to hear about something exotic, and it gives this black student a chance to explain his culture to the other students. I bet he never gets the chance to do that. He doesn't say a whole lot, but hey, what teenage boy does? He's such a good kid. I'm gonna give him at least a B+ for this class.

MORAL FOR RENTERS: Some rentals just don't do what you want them to do. Stick with the good ones.

RENTER: Jenny Smith, a senior at a predominantly white school
EVENT TYPE: Individual
LOCATION: Sports team training camp

The renter writes:
My name is Jenny and this is my first time officially renting a black person. I'm pretty excited. It all starts at dinner at my sports training camp. I'm sitting in the dining room all by myself at a table. I'm bored. I'm trying to imagine who will sit with me to make my dinner more exciting. Just as I think this, one of the black girls from the team walks in. I signal to our coach that I want her to sit with me and I see the coach pointing to my table and telling the black girl to sit with me.

There are two black girls on the team. The coach keeps getting their names mixed up. They play the same position, so there's only one of them on the field at a time and I guess it can get pretty confusing as to who is who. But I know the difference, 'cause one of them is really black and the other is kind of light brown. Plus, one has a strange name, something with a bunch of vowels and syllables that I can't always remember or pronounce. The other one has a normal name, Sandra. Anyway, I think they're both pretty interesting and I've always wanted to talk to one of them, so I'm excited when the coach tells this one (the one who isn't Sandra) to sit with me.

She sits down. She says she's really hungry, which I believe because at training camp we run two miles to the field and back twice a day, carrying our equipment. The sun is hot and practice is brutal. It's cool to be seen with her. The other girls are looking at our table curiously. They must be wondering what we're going to talk about. The girls at the table where the other black girl is sitting look at me and smile.

Dinner is served, and for a minute I am scared that I won't know what to talk about with a black girl. Then I feel the sting of my sunburn when the salt from my pasta touches my lips. I look at this girl across the table from me and her beautiful brown skin and I think of all her ancestors in the hot sun in Africa, and I immediately figure out that black people must not get sunburned! Wow, that must be so cool. I wish I was like that. I'm totally fascinated, so I ask her all about it. Now we will have plenty to talk about.

"Do you get tan? I am so fair skinned that I burn in the sun. I can't go out in the sun at all, but you don't have to worry about that, do you? You don't really call it 'tan,' though if you get darker or blacker, maybe you call it 'blacker.' Because 'tan' is a color, and you're already darker than tan. I mean, you're black."

She keeps eating as I talk to her. My thoughts keep coming, it's so cool. I totally can talk to black people, it's easy, even if I can't pronounce all of their names.

"You don't have to use any sunscreen I bet. That saves a lot of money. I mean you're used to the sun, all that sun in Africa and all. There's no sunscreen there. I wonder how dark can you get? Can you get as dark as this black napkin? Have you ever been that dark? Or maybe it doesn't affect you at all, you're already brown, you probably just stay that way. It must be so much easier for you, I have to spend all this time worrying about my skin, but for you being in the sun is natural."

This is so much fun. I can't wait to tell all my friends!

MORAL FOR RENTERS: Don't be afraid to talk to black people. It's easy!

RENTER: Mark Saunders, a musician in a rock band
EVENT TYPE: Individual/personal
LOCATION: Renter's grandmother's house
OTHER SERVICES: High question volume

The rental reflects:
I am on a rental retainer as the girlfriend to a guy in a rock band. Well, a pop/rock band. The music isn't great, but I like a couple of the

songs. Anyway, I'm not getting paid to be a fan, I'm getting paid to be black, and that's my specialty.

It's a year-long rental, so I'm psyched to charge a big fee. For the most part, the rental is pretty standard. I'm the new black girlfriend. Get this, he said he had a dream once where he was dating a black girl, and then I showed up and he thought it was fate. He says he's always wanted to date a black girl, and here I am.

His friends think he's pretty cool because he's dating me, and he likes to feel cooler than his friends, so I think he's pretty satisfied with the arrangement. None of them have ever been so daring as to date a black person. When we are together his friends make lots of comments about how he has always been the strange one, how he does oddball things, and is always off the beaten path. They compare our relationship to the time he dyed his hair blue, or the time he stopped eating for a week just to see what it felt like.

Today we are stopping by his grandmother's house for a visit before he heads out of town on tour. I walk into the house, and as he shows me around we pass through the kitchen and I notice a pair of salt and pepper shakers decorated to look like a black "mammy" and "uncle," both carrying trays to look like they are serving a meal as well as the salt or pepper that pours out of their heads. They are dressed in red, white, and yellow with coal-black faces and white gloves. I wonder how many times my renter had walked past those same salt and pepper shakers as he thought, "I always wanted to have a black girlfriend." I wonder if he thinks salt or pepper comes out of my head.

We sit down with his grandmother, who is watching a television talk show. It's Christmas and the host has a gospel choir on, singing songs of the season. The three of us sit and watch for quite a while in virtual silence. Suddenly his grandmother speaks in a grizzly voice, "Sure, when they're singing they're bouncing up and down, but try to get one of 'em to use a vacuum cleaner and then they've got no energy."

I almost spit out my eggnog, but I stop myself from laughing before I get nog up my nose. My "boyfriend" and I both turn our heads toward the older woman. My renter explains to his grandmother that the people on the television are singers, not cleaning people. I choke down my beverage and quietly excuse myself to the other room. I walk into the kitchen where I smile knowingly at the salt and pepper shakers. Times have really changed. At least now, I'm on the clock.

My renter follows me into the kitchen and quietly, so his grandmother doesn't hear, apologizes for her comment. He tells me that she meant young people, not black people—after all, the choir was only mostly black. He asks me not to say anything to her about it as she is old and doesn't understand what she has just said. "Hey, if that's what makes you comfortable. I've heard it all before." I say, "Buying my silence is going to cost you another $1,000 though." He'll have to wait to get that new guitar, but now I won't.

MORAL FOR RENTALS: Keep a running tab. You never know when Grandma is going to earn you a bonus check!

RENTER: Melissa Hanson, a former employee at a telecommunications company
EVENT TYPE: Individual/personal
LOCATION: A trendy diner
OTHER SERVICES: "Help, I need a black opinion!" and "Tell them I'm not a racist" vouch

The rental reflects:
I have been requested to meet a repeat renter for lunch. Usually this renter wants to chat about general things, mostly her love life, while she is seen in the company of a black person. She is young and image conscious. She thinks hanging out with a black girl brings style to her reputation. I usually hear from her about once a year, just enough to keep current with her black "friend." She's pretty enjoyable, and though she never seems to learn anything more about black people in the year between our visits, she's actually kind of fun to hang out with.

Today at lunch, things are pretty much as usual. We talk about basic things: work, relationships, the town I live in, the town she lives in. It's all about being seen together, so there's no need to get into deep conversations. After some small talk she says, "Oh, I wanted to ask you something. You're black, you might be able to help me with this." This is a new step for this renter who usually tends to avoid direct conversation about race. My curiosity is piqued. Actually, I'm pretty excited. When she asks me advice, it's usually about her love life, so I wonder if her question was going to be about a new black beau. My ears perk up and my mind begins to imagine the possibilities.

Before my mind can travel too far into voyeuristic territory, she jolts me back into reality. "So, like I was telling you, I just got laid off from my job. Anyway, there is this bunch of black people who work at my company. They all got laid off too." She whispers the word "black." Sometimes she substitutes "African American" but still in a whisper.

She goes on with her story. "One of them, this black woman, who had been pretty mean to me before, all of a sudden started being really nice to me. I've always been nice to her, and all the black people at the company. Of course I don't have anything against them because they are black. Anyway, I don't know why she would do this, but she took me to lunch. At lunch she started asking me all of these questions about the layoffs and the severance package I had negotiated. Then her cell phone beeped and she said 'Whoops, I think I have my phone on record.' Can you believe that? I think she was recording our conversation! I felt so violated, so used. I think she was the spokesperson or the investigator for the whole group of black people. They always hung together like a group at work. But I don't know why she would do that to me. I had always been nice to them. I don't understand her actions. So I thought I'd ask you. Why did she do that?"

I stare blankly at Melissa as my brain takes a detour to rewrite a popular 1980s tune: "Don't blame it on the sunshine. Don't blame it on the moonlight. Don't blame it on the good times. Blame it on the Blackie." I snap out of the momentary lapse into disco and gather my thoughts. It takes me a second since I know nothing about her company or the politics of the layoffs. I have never met the woman she was referring to and worried that I could not be of much help. From what my race-dar tells me, this woman's actions had nothing to do with her being black.

However, I am a professional and an experienced rental, and I find myself in this classic and sensitive situation frequently. When I have to say to a renter, "The problem you are dealing with is not related to race," it has to be put very delicately. Offering my official black opinion, I say, "You said that everyone at the company was pretty upset about the layoffs. This woman was probably just trying to find out if other people had negotiated better settlements. I'm sure lots of people of all races were having those kinds of conversations after the layoffs. You were probably not the only one she talked to. As a black person, but really, as a fellow worker, I'm sure she just wanted some information."

Realizing Melissa felt personally slighted by this woman's behavior, which was admittedly suspicious, I add, "Or maybe she was just a mean person." Melissa responds by saying, "It made me so uncomfortable. I had been so nice to her and all the black people, I didn't know why she would do that to me. Take me out to lunch and interrogate me like that."

MORAL: It's always about being black.

RENTER: Isabella Slate, artist and all-around creative type
EVENT TYPE: Individual/personal
LOCATION: A local café
OTHER SERVICES: "Tell them I'm not racist" vouch

The rental reflects:
This rental was a blast. I'm going to be telling stories about this for years to come. I met this woman in a coffee shop, as she requested. She wants to rent me "Because you and I are doing the same thing in

different ways." This means that deep inside she "feels black" and she wants me to validate her by sharing stories of how we're both in the trenches fighting the good fight for our race. My reply, "Yep, we sure are. You and me sister, two of a kind. That'll be $375."

I arrive early to do a little writing before the rental. As I sit in this coffee shop, I pick through my change to see if I have enough for a drink and a cookie. I come across one of those novelty quarters commemorating moments of American history from each state. This one is for New Hampshire. It says Live Free or Die.

I turn the quarter over in my fingers wondering when the quarter showing an enslaved black person picking cotton would be released into the currency system. I wonder if one of the southern states would display the motto Segregation Now! Maybe Texas would proudly post on their quarter Last to Free the Slaves.

My renter arrives.

She's very excited and starts talking right away. She barely says hello. Sure enough, she says exactly what I expected. She has always felt that she's more black than any other race she might choose. She's "certainly not white." Sometimes, even other people think she's black. She asks if I can explain this. I can't. She continues. She tells me she's a writer who just "writes what she knows." She says that some of the people she's submitted her work to actually think she's black. She doesn't know what to make of this. Except that she finds it odd. Later I learn that she's written a story called "I Am a Black Chick." She's the main character in the story. It's all about her. Maybe that's why people who read her work think she's black. Just a guess.

So far the rental is pretty easy, since I can't get much of a word in edgewise. I sit and listen, I still ponder the quarters, thinking up new mottos like Capitol of the Confederacy and The Home of Jim Crow. My renter continues with her stories. Now she's talking about how she takes a lot of flack from people for her work. Here's where she really wants to identify with me. She asks me if I find it hard, if people criticize me, and how I get by. Yes, people criticize me a lot. I sympathize. As for getting by . . . I'm not sure I am getting by, after all, I was just picking through my spare change to buy a cookie. I throw in an inclusive sounding sentence or two, "We all do what we can to keep going. You know how it is." She seems vindicated by my strategic choice of the word "we." This energizes her to talk more. I don't have to say much, she keeps the conversation alive pretty well on her own.

My mind is still designing currently. Florida's motto could be Denying Black People the Vote in 2000. Alabama's quarter might read Lynching Capitol of the U.S.—or is that Mississippi?

She says she feels unappreciated for her work, after all it isn't easy being as daring and controversial as she is. It's hard being a black writer these days. "You're so right." I say, "It must be so hard for you especially, being black in a white body and all." She attends conferences for writers of color and promotes her work. She says white people think she's trying to cause trouble and black people are suspicious of her. She seems to want me to thank her for being so courageous and daring. "Thanks," I say. "Where would we be without people like you telling the story of the black experience?" She gives me a big hug. I'm not sure if I'm joking or serious at this point. I don't know who I'm talking to. What if she really is black on the inside?

MORAL FOR RENTALS: Let the renter do the talking. You can make a bundle just saying yes and smiling.

RENTER: University alumni group
EVENT TYPE: Nonprofit gathering
LOCATION: The restaurant of a successful alum of the college
OTHER SERVICES: High question volume

The renter writes:
This is so great. I am in a pinch for a luncheon and need some people of color there. I have one Asian American and one Latino American but I need an African American. Thankfully there is one for rent through my alumni group. Perfect.

When my rental arrives I immediately give her a big hug and introduce her to every single person in the room. Then I sit her next to the guest speaker, a visitor from our college, in town to discuss general issues with local alumni. I run to the photographer to tell him to make sure he gets as many photos of the three people of color as possible. It looks so good to the school when we send in photos of a diverse group.

Today we have such a great opportunity with the guest speaker here and three people of color to talk about diversity at our university. I initiate a serious discussion about the low numbers of minority students enrolling at the school. It's such a mystery to most of us in the room. We explore several creative reasons to explain the dearth of color on campus.

Soon a brilliant answer is discovered. The guest speaker suggests that many black kids don't even know about colleges. He proposes that "They and their parents have never even heard of schools like us." He talks at length and with great enthusiasm about this idea. Everyone agrees and praises his remarkable insight.

This is where the rentals come in. We need them to validate our ideas. The guest speaker turns to the black person and says, "Isn't that true? I bet your parents had never even heard of our school before you went there."

Without even a pause, she responds. "Actually, my parents had made it very clear from the time I could read that I would go to the best school the country had to offer. Like any ambitious student I worked to prepare myself for college" . . . blah . . . blah . . . blah . . . "even taking the SAT when I was in seventh grade."

We are all a bit shocked. None of us had considered this answer. Now we're all a bit embarrassed. Not only does she shoot down our idea but she is pretty snobbish in the process. That just seems unnecessary. To add insult to injury, the Asian and Latino American seem to be chuckling under their breath at the whole thing. Then the guest speaker finds an excuse to remove himself from the conversation. I think he says he needs to hit the buffet again. I am mortified, but I know the food is good. At least the caterer did his job as ordered.

For the rest of the luncheon the guest speaker seems uncomfortable. His conversations with the people of color are brief and he often leaves after a few polite remarks. Earlier he had hinted at inviting our group to a couple of national events and now I think we'll never get invited.

MORAL FOR RENTERS: Tell your rentals what you expect in advance. Give them a script if necessary.

RENTER: Officer Michael Allens
EVENT TYPE: Impulse rental
LOCATION: A street at night

The rental reflects:
This is a surprise rental. Cops often rent on the fly. I guess I asked for it, because I had a broken headlight that I just hadn't gotten around to fixing. I just looked at it one too many times and said to myself, "You've got to get that fixed or it's going to cause a problem."

Anyway, I'm driving home from a movie with my white friend Jay. We have a habit of seeing really bad movies together. Usually some adventure flick with spies and guns and a completely unrealistic plot. It's fun, a little break from reality from time to time. Anyway, we're driving back from the movie when a police car signals to me to pull over. I'm in the driver's seat and Jay is next to me. Jay sits through those bad movies with me even though he hates violence of all kinds, even when it's not real. Needless to say, Jay is freaking out.

I'm not so worried, because this is the third or fourth time I've gotten stopped by a police officer recently. Then there was the time a cop in a car followed me through a neighborhood when I was riding my bicycle. That was fascinating. He kept weaving back and forth slowly behind me, beside me, across my path. He never stopped me but he spent a good deal of time following me. I never figured that one out. What damage could I do on my bike? Maybe my dorky maroon backpack was suspicious looking. After that, I stuck an American flag on my backpack and now I pretty much bike around town unbothered.

Anyway, so this cop pulls me over for an insta-rental. These are always tricky because the police officers aren't usually in the best mood, so it can be hard to get them to pay for the rental. I'm compiling a running tab to send to the police department on an annual basis.

I also know that with Jay in the car next to me the police officer is going to be disappointed. He won't be able to really rough me up or scare me as is traditional. I hand him my license and registration and try to calm down Jay while the cop goes back to check me out.

"Did you know that 'cop' stands for 'constable on patrol?' It's of British origin." I say to Jay, trying to distract him from this tense situation. I guess he doesn't get stopped by police officers that much. This might be a new experience for him.

The police officer returns, obviously frustrated that a white person is in the car with me and interfering with his rental opportunity. He gives me a warning and tells me to fix my headlight. Before he lets us go, he says sternly, "I assume you're going to drive your friend here home, and go back to where you live." Even though Jay and I live two blocks from each other, I don't argue. Last year a cop shot a black guy to death while he was sitting in his car with the seatbelt on. Ouch, that's one rental I don't want to do. I'm excited that I'm getting off pretty easy. I think I won't even charge the police department for this one. The next week, Jay fixes my headlight.

MORAL FOR RENTALS: Travel with white friends at night. They really come in handy!

RENTER: Johnny Santoro, the director of an important theatre company
EVENT TYPE: Nonprofit event
LOCATION: Wherever the right person is spotted
OTHER SERVICES: A "black accent" is necessary

The renter writes:
I am producing a play that deals with serious issues. It centers around a white family and their child who is going to college and struggling with becoming an adult. The family has a black housekeeper who has been a really important figure in the young man's life. She doesn't have a lot of lines, but she is critical to the development of the other characters. I need to find a black woman or a black man in drag to play the role.

I am at a friend's wedding when I spot the perfect person to play the part. I noticed her when the groom was saying his vows. She was crying softly in her seat. She was so tough and sensitive at the same time. I'm hoping I don't have to actually rent this black woman for the part, since I'm a poor artist and can barely pay myself. I'm hoping she'll be flattered by my attention and be thrilled to say yes.

The reception is a small and friendly gathering so I'm sure she won't mind my coming up and asking her if she'll audition for me. The bride is about to toss the bouquet to the unmarried women in the room. This seems like as good a time as any to talk to the black woman about my play. She is just about to leave her seat when I tap her on the shoulder. Whew, I almost lost my chance.

I sit down next to her. She looks toward the bouquet tossing for a moment, but I grab her attention by saying, "I am directing a play and I have a role that you would be perfect for. I really, really want you to consider doing it. You are perfect for the part."

She looks from me to the bride and back to me. I continue. "It is a great play, by a classic playwright. It was just revived on Broadway and is going to be the hottest thing this town has seen. It tackles some really serious issues, exactly the kind of things I know you are into."

I know I've caught her attention now, but just to make sure, I tell her more.

"The role is really fantastic. She's a black woman. She's probably been poor, and seen some hard times in her life. The script doesn't really say, but I think that makes sense. Now she is very close with this family and has been almost a mother to their son, who is leaving the nest to become an independent man. She is such an important character in the play. It almost revolves around her. She really is the central character in the show."

The bouquet flies and women scream in the background.

"I want to cast her in a way that is totally different than she's ever been done before and I think you'd be great for it. You have a really contemporary look and that's what I'm going for. I want to show that she's a modern person, even though she is a housekeeper. But really she is more like a second mother in the family. When the son leaves, she loses a part of herself.

"I want her to have an 'edge,' and you're really edgy and tough. I know you could play her because you're such a strong, tough, funky person. Can you look and sound really 'urban?' Where did you grow up? I want her to have an urban flair. She's the kind of woman who 'don't take no attitude,' just like you. But I want her to be nurturing too. She's got to be a compassionate character. She should remind the audience members of their favorite auntie. So what do you think? Can you do it?"

She takes a long look at me, and though she's only five feet two I have to admit, I'm scared of her. Yet at the same time, I wish she would bring her funky black sass over to my house. I can just see her telling my son, "You crazy boy! You better eat all your peas or I'll give you a whuppin'!" She doesn't even need to audition. She's going to be perfect—I can just tell by looking at her. My play is going to be a smash hit.

MORAL FOR RENTERS: You never know when you're going to need to rent on the spot. Carry extra cash.

Through the Looking Glass:
The Future of Renting a Negro

The future of any business depends on the continued commitment of its clients. The consumers in any successful market must express a loyalty for the goods and services exchanged. This insures the sustainability of the demand for those services. If the demand for rent-a-negro services continues to grow and thrive the way it has for the past several decades, the market is sure to have a long life and expand. It has been an integral part of our global economy for years and has adapted to modern needs as skillfully as the demand for many other valuable natural resources. Renting is ready to take on the future at full steam, thanks to the dedication of consumers all over the world.

Even though the upward trend for renting is strong, history has seen markets respond to historical events, public opinion, and consumer focus. Only you can ensure a solid future for the business of renting. Ask yourself, what am I doing every day already that helps keep the rental business thriving? Every little gesture helps keep the business of renting alive and booming. If you don't tend to the little things you do each day that sustain the business, the market might suffer and dwindle. Without renting, how will people learn how to interact with each other? Keep this in mind as you go through your day.

At this moment, however, there isn't much fear that the market will suffer any great losses or setbacks. There have been some dips in the business, even a scare or two that the market might bottom out. But at every turn, the demand for renting has proven to be resilient, perhaps one of the most resilient and adaptable demand-driven markets in the history of commerce. Renters' reliance on the availability of rentals is virtually unflappable. With this kind of dedication, renting will evolve for generations. Don't miss out on long-term investments. Start now by training your children in the basics of renting and being rented. We all have to work together to keep this sacred practice intact.

Dear Negro:
Letters to rent-a-negro.com

At rent-a-negro.com we have received thousands of e-mails from inquisitive citizens interested in our services. Sometimes these e-mails express some concern or distress at the nature of our business. Many people have requested a gander at these e-mails and responses to the site. Look no further. Here, published for the first time, are just a few of our favorite letters received at rent-a-negro.com.

Dear Rent-a-Negro:

You should be ashamed of yourself! This is worse than slavery!

Signed,
I'm Ashamed for You

Dear Ashamed:

Now come on. It's not really worse than slavery. Wouldn't you rather be paid for the countless times you've been asked if your hair is real, or if you can give dance lessons? It's not quite the same as being chained, starved, and overworked while living in subhuman conditions and healing from your latest whipping. Really, when you compare the two, I doubt you'd choose slavery. But I'd bet you are being rented on a daily basis without suitable wages. Actually, now that you point it out, maybe your life is a little bit like slavery: working all those hours, for someone else's benefit, without pay or recognition. You might want to take a look at that.

Dear Rent-a-Negro:

I am white, and I went to your Web site rent-a-negro.com. How do you expect racial tranquility when you promote such an idea? Yes, many white people do not know anything personal about black people. You claim that this service helps white people to understand blacks. In fact I would argue the opposite. By having this service where human beings are rented out, you are making black people seem like an exotic delicatessen for white people. Blacks are made into an exhibit. "Touch her skin, touch her hair." $25. I don't think that most white people are sitting around in their houses wondering what a black person's hair feels like. You seem to be anti-white.

Signed,
Ayo Should Go Byo

Dear Byo:

I'm not anti-white. Some of my closest friends are white. I have a great deal of respect for white people. I am actually quite comfortable around them. I watch white television shows all the time. I've read white books, and I even saw a movie last year starring all white people and it was very good.

You are right that most white people are not sitting around wondering what a black person's hair feels like. Many of them are out on the streets, in stores, on busses, in public restrooms, and in bars, finding out firsthand what a black person's hair feels like. Many of them have found out by grabbing my hair. No, I didn't create the "exotic delicatessen." Many white people approach me with their taste buds already on overdrive.

This is ayo, going byo . . .

Dear Rent-a-Negro:

Thanks for creating rent-a-negro!

You have really brought attention to this issue. I, too, have lived through the "can I touch your hair" episodes in my life; so much so that it has altered my life and has taken a piece of my soul. Whenever a white person touched my hair, I don't care if it was my dearest friend in the world . . . they would instinctively wipe their hands on their pants leg. Oh . . . I've been through that time and time again. It's to the point now that I have scant dealings with whites because of their inherent attitude towards us.

Rent-a-negro, in my opinion, is your way and, in a sense, black people's way of wiping *our* hands on *our* pants leg.

Thank you so much!!

Sincerely,
Now My Hands Are Clean

Dear Clean Hands:

Thank you for your letter. It is one of my favorites. It might help you to carry an invoice on you at all times. The next time a person touches your hair, you can collect a fee. You might want to add a handkerchief or a napkin as a kind gesture to the renter. That way, after they're done touching your hair, they won't have to soil their pants legs. Best of luck!

Dear Rent-a-Negro:

Imagine the slave trade never existed. Where would you be? It is unfortunate but I believe your ancestors suffering paved the way for your ability to live in the U.S.A. Not many Africans could afford to leave their homeland to seek a new life in America. So, I suspect that had your ancestors not been hunted down and sold to the slave trade, by other Africans, you could possibly be a mother of a malnutritioned/starving child in a third world African country.

Remember this . . . we aren't here for a long time, we're here for a good time. Try to make the best of what you have to work with and try to make those around you smile.

Peace,
Here for a Good Time

Dear Good Time:

OK. I'm imagining the slave trade never existed. (Hang on, this might take a minute. It did last over 200 years.) Hmm . . . Ah, yes . . . now I see it. Darn! White people are still asking me simplistic and obvious questions about being black. OK. Let me try again (I'm concentrating hard this time). Sh*t! White people are still holding me back in school and requiring me to prove my intelligence twice as much as what they require of my white peers. OK. One more try. (Deep breaths, focus . . .) Ah, there it is. White people are treating me entirely as an equal, sharing economic growth and offering me and my ancestors an equal profit in the history and future of this country. Gee, I love my integrated neighborhood. And my house—it's huge. Wow, someone pinch me, I must be dreaming. Oh, right, I am.

I did like the visions of rich white people picking their own cotton, though. Thanks for that one.

Dear Rent-a-Negro:

The service you provide is your personal business. However I think you could have come up with a better name that the one you chose. Please respond. I am curious why you as an educated person would use such a name for your site. I have come up with some ideas as to why; but I would like to hear your reasoning.

Is this some type of sick joke—or are you lost in your identity?

Can you be a little more creative?

Or are you just an idiot?

I will never support your organization.

You are literally disgusting and should not have been born.

I think people like you should be ashamed to live.

Might I suggest that you just hike your skirt; bend over; and continue to get screwed in your—well you know the rest—perhaps.

Sincerely,
Someone who does not think your website is neither funny nor productive. What happened you couldn't find better things to do with your time. You are disgusting.

Dear Someone Who Does Not Think My Web Site is Neither Funny Nor Productive:

Well now, didn't your cordial letter quickly deteriorate into insults and vulgarities? I'm so glad you found a way to get all that nastiness out. Do you feel better? Good. Happy to be of service. That will be $150.

Dear Rent-a-Negro:

Is this a joke? How can someone be so hard pressed for money or media coverage to do such a thing. If you want to sell your time that's your personal business, but to drag down the African American community with you is pathetic.

Signed,
Wishing for a Retraction

Dear Retraction:

Really? I am dragging down the entire African American community? I had no idea. I have heard that the black community is susceptible to total and complete deterioration as a result of one person's actions. But I've noticed that there are countless white murderers, rapists, imperial dictators, war criminals, serial murderers, corrupt officials, homicidal and genocidal maniacs, and through it all the white community has managed to stay afloat. How do they do it?

Dear Rent-a-Negro:

I am shocked that this service exists. Do you realize why selling African Americans was outlawed? Because it is wrong. If a white person is scared to be around black people, they shouldn't be around them. I am a white person and I respect all black people. Most of the black people I know aren't scary at all. They are just like all other people—white, Hispanic, Chinese, Vietnamese, Mexican. Everyone is alike.

Signed,
Shocked But No Longer Scared

Dear Shocked:

You truly are a representative of our fine society. Your open-minded perspective is keenly in touch with popular opinion. Thanks for sharing.

Dear Rent-a-Negro:

Quick question.

Why is it that it's always you privileged, Ivy League, lighter-skinned/not so negro-looking ones remarking and harping on the mundane facts of the color line?

Just wondering.

Signed,
Do You Have a Brown Bag Handy?

Dear Brown Bag,

Upon receiving your e-mail, I sent it to my mother, who is often a source of wisdom for myself and others. Here is her response:

> "Surely you know that it has often been the 'light-skinned negroes' who systemically broke down barriers and opened doors so black people, regardless of skin shade, could seize opportunity.
>
> Separating ourselves according to skin shade is a practice established by slave masters. Certainly, we as a people do not want to perpetuate that thought process."

Aw, Mom. She's the best.

Dear Rent-a-Negro:

It is true that white man once owned black man due to the fact that white man had the superior weapons and black man was inferior in his ability to defend himself. White man apologized and black man caught up, at least black man out of Africa. I shake my head in confusion. White man already pay reparations, it is called welfare.

Thank you.

Signed,
Shake My Head
P.S. Write back if you dare. :)

Dear Truth or Dare:

If you do a little research you'll find that the majority of welfare recipients in this country are white. Thus I don't think you can count welfare payments as reparations for African American slavery.

And can you send me a copy of the white man's apology for once owning black man? I'd love to frame that and hang it on my wall.

Dear Rent-a-Negro:

Hi. I need to rent a negro, and your service is a good one, but you are far to light to be considered a true "negro." I would say you are more of a mulatto, or, as we in the south would say a "high yeller," and on occasion, you'd be described as a black "with a little cream in your coffee." I need a much darker negro. If you can find me one willing to work in the "rent-a-negro" fashion. I could really use a good negro to impress my upper class white clients by keeping a negro around as my "hip black friend." Most white liberals I encounter, while preaching equality and tolerance, have seldom seen a negro up close, and it would be a new experience for them. I simply need this option to wow my rich white clients. But there is the problem of that light skin you have.

Signed,
I Take My Coffee Black

Dear Black Coffee:

Well, you certainly have a particular preference. I am always pleased to hear from someone who knows exactly what they want. A decisive consumer does make a better customer. As for your concerns, I assure you, though I am light skinned, I am indeed black. I'm sure I could fulfill your request. From what I can tell, my light skin has not prevented me from serving as an authentic black person. But if you truly prefer darker-skinned blacks, you might conduct your own search for an independent contractor who is black enough to meet your needs. I'm sure you'll find someone satisfactory.

Hello Rent-a-Negro:

My son and I just recently visited your Web site. We are interested to know why you named the site rent-a-negro. We thought as African Americans you might change the name to something more suitable and professional.

Here are some of our suggestions: Afro-Conversations, The Meeting Place, Race Relations, Talk to Me, Cultural Expressions, to name a few.

Don't get me wrong, we like the business idea, but not the site name.

Thank you for your time and God bless you in your endeavors.

Signed,
Mother and Son

Dear Mother and Son:

Thanks for the tip. It's so nice to see a parent and child working on a project together. Maybe you should open a rental business under one of the names you suggested! Maybe you can even call it Rental and Son: Cultural Expressions, or something like that. Multigenerational rentals are a big hit at community picnics and school board meetings. Good luck!

Dear Rent-a-Negro:

This is so racist.

I'm outraged at the blatant racism of your "Rent-A-Negro" site. If you're not going to offer Asian or Arab rental as well, you should at least provide information on how people could get in touch with such services.

And also, some of my best friends are black!

Signed,
With a Deep Sense of Injustice

Dear Injustice:

I get this request a lot. You'll notice, however, that rent-a-negro principles have been applied to all people of color for many years, with much the same impact. It should not be too difficult to find Asian, Arab, Latino, and indigenous people working as unpaid rentals all over the world. I'm sure they would be happy to be compensated for their work.

Dear Rent-a-Negro:

I filled out the online form and I selected that I have indeed paid for services rendered by negroes before. In fact every time I've use negroes I've paid.

I've never used your service, yet I get a message that "your" records indicate that I have not paid. This simply isn't true. I would appreciate a response explaining your contention about my never paying for services. I would also like to add that I've always paid well! Above union scale in fact.

Hope to hear from you soon.

Wealthy Guy, Unnamed Corporation

Dear Wealthy:

It is rare for the site to malfunction. Take a look at your records. Are you certain you've always paid the asking price for the services rendered you from all of the African Americans in your life? Think about it. Was it that time you tried to pick up that black woman with that little white lie about having black friends? Was it the moment you called the bartender "brotha"? Could it have been your last corporate event where there was only one black attendee in a pool of white faces? I bet if you think hard enough, you'll remember something. By the way, this advice cost $75. Please send your check in the mail.

Dear Rent-a-Negro:

In the interest of fairness and equality I think you should offer the same services to African Americans who would like to have a token honky at the event of their choice. I for one would love to help the cause of diversity by helping you launch rent-a-whitey. Please let me know if this exciting new service would mesh with your existing service.

Signed,
I Want My Piece of the Pie

Dear Pie Dicer:

If you find a demand for the service you describe, by all means launch it. You may want to wait for the majority of African Americans to have the financial means to pay for such a service, as many are still attempting to recoup their own overdue rental fees.

About the Author

damali ayo has been a professional black person for more than thirty years. A conceptual artist and the creator of rent-a-negro.com, ayo and her work have been featured in Salon.com, *Washington Post*, *Chicago Tribune*, the *Wall Street Journal*, and *Harper's Magazine*.

For more information on damali ayo's conceptual artwork and shows, or to join her e-mail list, please visit http://damaliayo.com.

On the Real Side
A History of African American Comedy
By Mel Watkins

"Fascinating and exhaustive . . . at once a serious
social history and an enormously entertaining
reading experience."—*Chicago Tribune*

"A penetrating and immensely enjoyable history
. . . . For many readers, this book will transform
their conception of the character, and the source,
of much American popular culture."
   —*The New Yorker*

This comprehensive history of black humor sets it in the context of American
popular culture. Blackface minstrelsy, Stepin Fetchit, and the Amos 'n' Andy
show presented a distorted picture of African Americans; this book contrasts
this image with the authentic underground humor of African Americans
found in folktales, race records, and all-black shows and films. After generations of stereotypes, the underground humor finally emerged before the
American public with Richard Pryor in the 1970s. But Pryor was not the first
popular comic to present authentically black humor. Watkins offers surpris-
ing reassessments of such seminal figures as Fetchit, Bert Williams, Moms
Mabley, and Redd Foxx, looking at how they paved the way for contemporary comics such as Whoopi Goldberg, Eddie Murphy, and Bill Cosby.

PAPER $16.95 (CAN $25.95)
672 PAGES 1556523513

Available at your favorite bookstore or by calling (800) 888-4741.

Lawrence Hill Books
www.lawrencehillbooks.com

Distributed by Independent Publishers Group
www.ipgbook.com

African American Humor

The Best Black Comedy from Slavery to Today

Edited by Mel Watkins,
Foreword by Dick Gregory

"Mel Watkins has done for comedy
what Alex Haley did for the family."
—Ishmael Reed

"Full of raucous mirth."
—*American Legacy*

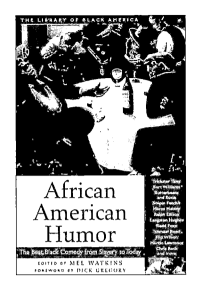

This collection of anecdotes, tales, jokes, toasts, rhymes, satire, riffs, poems, stand-up sketches, and snaps documents the evolution of African American humor over the past two centuries. It includes routines and writings from such luminaries as Bert Williams, Butterbeans & Susie, Stepin Fetchit, Moms Mabley, Ralph Ellison, Langston Hughes, Redd Foxx, Ishmael Reed, Bill Cosby, Richard Pryor, Martin Lawrence, and Chris Rock. This anthology includes classic stage routines, literary examples, and witty quotations presented in their entirety.

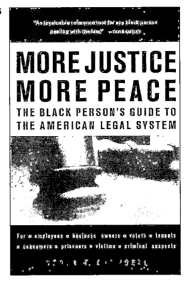

The Colors of Love
The Black Person's Guide to Interracial Relationships
By Kimberly Hohman

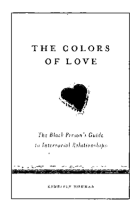

"The fight against racism is waged many ways. This book tells the tale of people who challenge it one person and one relationship at a time. The development of a human ethic that embraces the human spirit in all its variety will emerge from their example."—Carol Moseley Braun

"Practical advice, by the book, for the bridal couple." —Associated Press

PAPER $14.95 (CAN $22.95)
208 PAGES 1556524676

Working While Black
The Black Person's Guide to Success in the White Workplace
By Michelle T. Johnson

"This book examines in an insightful way a delicate and difficult issue—the triumph and tragedies of black upward mobility. Don't miss it!" —Cornel West, author of *Race Matters*

"Employment attorney Johnson has plenty of good advice for African Americans on how to excel among white co-workers."—*Library Journal*

PAPER $14.95 (CAN $22.95)
218 PAGES 1556525109

Available at your favorite bookstore or by calling (800) 888-4741.

Lawrence Hill Books
www.lawrencehillbooks.com

Distributed by Independent Publishers Group
www.ipgbook.com